English Isn't, Crazy!

English Isn't Crazy!

*The Elements of Our Language
and How to Teach Them*

Diana Hanbury King
Fellow, Academy of Orton-Gillingham Practitioners and Educators

pro·ed
An International Publisher

8700 Shoal Creek Boulevard
Austin, Texas 78757-6897
800/897-3202   Fax 800/397-7633
www.proedinc.com

© 2000 by Diana Hanbury King
Published by PRO-ED, Inc.
8700 Shoal Creek Boulevard
Austin, Texas 78757-6897
800/897-3202   Fax 800/397-7633
www.proedinc.com

Typography Type Shoppe II Productions Ltd.
Cover design by Joseph Dieter.

New to this edition are maps presented at the end of the book.

ISBN-13: 978-141640091-3
ISBN-10: 1-4164-0081-8

Previously published by York Press, Inc. under ISBN 0-912752-59-9.

Printed in the United States of America

4 5 6 7 8 9 10 11 12 13   17 16 15 14 13

For Kurt, Joan, Marie, and Steve
without whom none of these dreams
would have materialized.

CONTENTS

PREFACE

My own interest in language started at an early age in England, where I was taught by governesses, first German and then French. By the time I was nine, my sister and I were conversing in three languages. In college I added Italian and majored in comparative Germanic philology. My career, however, led me elsewhere, for I spent my professional life in schools teaching English—essentially reading and writing skills—to students of various ages. Yet I never ceased to use the knowledge acquired early in life and always taught vocabulary and spelling in conjunction with word origins. Since my retirement, I have trained teachers, mostly in the New York State Public School system, and find that many of them share my love of words and want to know more.

This book is designed as an introduction for the elementary or secondary teacher whose preparation did not include the history and development of our language. I have interwoven important and interesting historical events that have led to the shaping of English with the changes that have occurred over time.

Practical suggestions for applying this knowledge with students of any age have been placed in the appendices of this book for ready reference. Included are suggestions of specific techniques that will make teaching this material effective. This book can also be read by motivated high school students.

It is my hope that teachers will be encouraged to explore this fascinating subject on their own and perhaps even to pick up a bilingual edition of Chaucer's *Canterbury Tales* or of Seamus Heaney's new translation of *Beowulf.* For further reading I recommend Bryson's eminently readable *Mother Tongue,* McCrum, Cran, and MacNeil's *The Story of English* and the new edition of the scholarly book, *The Origins and Development of the English Language* by Pyles and Algeo. Somewhat more detailed and specific are Robert Claiborne's *The Roots of English*, Miriam Balmuth's *Roots of Phonics*, and the erudite *An Introduction to Language* (with delightful cartoons) by Fromkin and Rodman. John Ayto's *Dictionary of Word Origins* is engaging and accessible to students. All the above are listed in my bibliography.

INTRODUCTION

You know this language that we speak,
Is part German, part Latin, and part Greek.
                        Peter, Paul, and Mary

English is rapidly becoming the most widely used language in the world. It has a vast number of speakers: an estimated 343 million, an additional 350 million for whom English is a second language, and perhaps as many as a billion who are learning it as a foreign language. Speakers of English now exceed those of Mandarin Chinese. Thus English is well on its way to becoming a universal language. For centuries, Latin was the common language of European peoples; it was the language of the Church, and it continues to be taught in schools and universities in the twenty-first century. French has long been the language of diplomacy. So, you may wonder, how is it that the language of a small island attained such importance?

In part, the spread of the British Empire, on which, at its height, the sun never set, accounts for the dominance of English. The Industrial Revolution was another factor. But there are other more recent elements at work: the tourist trade, which continues to be dominated by American travelers; radio and television; Hollywood's position in the film industry; World Wars I and II, as well as the conflicts in Korea and Vietnam (American servicemen took their language to the countries in which they served). World wide, English is the language used by pilots to communicate with controllers, and it is the language of computers and of scientific research (Pyles and Algeo 1993, 233).

But there is another factor. English has the largest vocabulary of any language—well over 650,000 words (of which about 200,000 are in common use). By contrast, German has 184,000 words and French and Russian fewer than 100,000 each (Bryson 1990, 13). English has amassed this vast vocabulary by its capacity to absorb elements from other languages. Never have the English tried to keep out foreign elements, as have the Germans (e.g., by making such substitutions as *Fernsprecher* "distance speaker" for *Telephon*) and the French, who even have an academy charged with maintaining the purity of the language. Recently the French announced a ban on English for official use. Currently there are 3,600 words the French are not supposed to use in school or government. A *walkman* is to be called a *balladeur*, and a *jumbo jet*, a *gros porteur*. Outlawed are words such as *beefsteak, on-line, brainstorming, bulldozer, airbag, log on*, and *makeup*.

For those of us who are teachers, the very richness of our language complicates our task. When we teach English, we are not teaching one but at least four languages. Even though scholars classify English as a Germanic language, Germanic, Teutonic, or Anglo-Saxon (the terms are synonymous) actually accounts for less than one percent of our language. But this one percent includes all the most common and familiar words. English idioms use the Anglo-Saxon forms. Thus we ask, "Why on *earth* did you do that?" We talk of something past as "*water* over the dam," and we say of an enthusiast that he is "all *fired* up." All the words on the Dolch list of "sight words" are of Germanic origin, as are all the words on any list of high-frequency words. Anglo-Saxon words are short, often contain silent letters, and present problems for both reading and spelling to a greater extent than do the more phonetically regular words of Latin and Greek origins. Latin words, over half of the English language, are longer and often composed of prefixes, roots, and suffixes. Greek words are the most abstract and scientific sounding and account for about ten percent of the words we use. Compare *earth*, *fire*, and *water* with the Latin *terrain*, *ignite*, and *aquatic* and with the Greek *geographic*, *pyre*, and *hydrogen*, and you will begin to get the idea of a language that moves from concrete to abstract. (For a listing of these elements, see Appendix F). You can make the same comparisons with any set of common Anglo-Saxon words and the Greek and Latin derivatives, e.g.,

Anglo-Saxon	Latin	Greek
star	*stellar*	*astronomy*
sun	*solarium*	*helium*
man	*virile*	*anthropology*
woman	*feminine*	*misogynist*

Germanic, Latin, and Greek words do not account for all the words we use; many words are derived from other languages or are of unknown origin.

French words have been entering our language since the Norman Conquest. In British schools, French was introduced to children at an early age; in this country its teaching has recently been widely displaced by Spanish language instruction. French words are numerous and challenging to teachers because they pose problems for both reading and spelling. Fortunately, for the most part, they constitute an advanced and sophisticated vocabulary not needed by young children. They are best taught to younger children on a need-to-know basis. However, they are important for high school and college students (see Appendix F).

Because the languages that form the basis of English are so different, they need to be approached in different ways. English is not "crazy," but it is highly complex, and English words reflect their origins by having their own structure and phonology. In general, the Anglo-Saxon elements are the first to be learned by young readers. But by the time children reach the fourth grade, they begin to encounter the Latin words in their social studies and science texts, and by high school they need to master the Greek-derived terminology of science courses. So it is that students should start to become familiar with Latin prefixes and roots in fourth grade and with Greek elements in seventh and eighth grades.

The reasons for the extraordinarily large vocabulary of English lie buried in the history of the language, and if we are to understand and appreciate our language, we have to begin with its history. A teacher equipped with knowledge of the history and elements of our language can enrich any lesson with information about words and their origins

ORIGINS

To gain an understanding of our language, we must journey far back in time.

Man is very old. Neanderthal man goes back to over 250,000 years and was followed by *Homo sapiens*, who seems to have evolved in Africa some 200 thousand years ago. About 30 thousand years ago *Homo sapiens* spread through the Near East and, following the retreat of the last Ice Age, on northward into Europe. At this time the body underwent certain important changes; the most significant for our purposes was that the larynx moved deeper into the throat, a physical change that made speech possible.

Not only did *Homo sapiens* have the larynx in the right place; he also possessed the necessary neurological apparatus for speech and an equally important prerequisite, an inner compulsion to communicate, to express himself, and to relate to other members of his community. Thus, language probably developed repeatedly in different times and places.

1

You may remember the discovery of the Iceman who was uncovered in Switzerland in 1991 and you may have been fascinated by the tools and accouterments found with him and the ingenuity and craftsmanship they reflected. The Iceman belonged to one of the groups that populated Europe in the early Indo-European period. The wonderful drawings in the caves at Lascaux in France and at Altamira in Spain date back to an even earlier time.

The early Indo-Europeans, whose language is the common ancestor of many languages, are thought to have originated in the region near the Black Sea, in modern day Ukraine. Other scholars believe they originated in the Danube valley, or perhaps at the edge of the Baltic Sea. We do not know exactly where they came from, but scholars have studied not only language, but also archaeology and myth in an attempt to learn more about these people. There is evidence that they had horses and perhaps chariots. They seem to have been herdsmen rather than farmers. Scholars have determined that they had words for *horse, bear, goat, ox, hare, hedgehog, salmon,* and *rabbit;* for *snow, thunder,* and *fire* (but not for *sea*); for *oak, beech, birch,* and *willow*; and for body parts—*eye, ear, heart,* and *foot* (Bryson 1993, 31).

Between 3500 and 2500 before the common era (B.C.E.), these Indo-Europeans, a patriarchal society, aggressive and warlike, began to migrate. They spread to central Asia and throughout Europe and, as they spread, they took their language with them. Their speakers moved to the east, even as far as western China; Tocharian, an extinct language, is Indo-European. As they moved, they split into many language groups, including Celtic, Germanic, Italic, Greek, Indo-Iranian, and Slavic. And, like the branches of a tree, these in turn subdivided. Indo-European languages are spoken by over half the population of the earth (Potter 1959, 84).

English belongs to one of these groups, the Germanic family. This group consisted originally of three subgroups: the northern, Scandinavian languages; the western, English, German, and Dutch; and an eastern branch, Gothic, which died out and is preserved only in early written records.

THE CELTS

During the early Neolithic times, about five thousand B.C.E., England was inhabited by roving bands of hunters who had moved north following the retreat of the last Ice Age. About a thousand years later, there began a wave of immigrations from the Continent. The Picts, small men and women, crossed the sea in little boats, dugouts and coracles—round boats made of skins stretched over a frame woven of wicker. Unlike the hunters, who had depended for their livelihood on whatever they could trap, catch, or kill, the Picts cleared the land, grew crops, domesticated animals, made flint tools, and baked pottery.

Around two thousand B.C.E., yet another wave of immigrants came to England from what is now Holland and the Rhineland. They were taller than the tribes that preceded them and had light brown hair. These were the Beaker Folk, who got their name from the bell-shaped drinking cups which they buried with their dead. They were the builders of the original Stonehenge.

About 1500 B.C.E., more people came from the Continent and built settlements, until the population grew to about one million within a hundred years. Then, at the beginning of the late Bronze Age, a new set of immigrants arrived, taller and stronger and armed with the skill to forge weapons of bronze. These builders and craftsmen eventually became known as the Wessex Culture (Hibbert 1992,14). They came and rebuilt Stonehenge with immense blocks of stone which they squared and dressed. These early people were sun worshipers. They may have been Druids. Eventually they disappeared, absorbed by the Celts, but they live on in the Celtic legends as the "little people" or faeries. A frequent theme in these early legends is their fear of iron, and it was iron in the hands of the Celts that led to their extinction.

At the beginning of the Iron Age, about 800 B.C.E., the Celts arrived in England from the Continent. Caesar referred to groups of tribes that occupied the land between the Pyrenees and the Rhine as the Aquitani, the Gauls, and the Belgae, but they were all Celts. The Celts were a branch of the Indo-Europeans who originated in Asia Minor. They were the first of the Indo-Europeans to spread over Europe and they settled in France, Belgium, and Germany, as well as in Spain and Italy. Both Dundee (Scotland) and Belgrade (Yugoslavia) are Celtic names.

The Celts had blue eyes and flaming red hair, and they cultivated flowing mustaches. But despite their fearsome appearance, they were far from being the barbarians that Roman propaganda would have had one believe. They lived in round wooden huts of clay-covered wattle with thatched roofs and they farmed the land, which they divided into square fields separated by banks. They plowed with oxen and grew oats, wheat, barley, and rye, and ground grain for bread. They drank mead made by fermenting a mixture of water and honey. They wore brightly colored clothing, especially red, and leather shoes and sandals. The wealthy wore fine brooches, bracelets, necklaces, and rings, often adorned with birds and animals in beautiful curvilinear designs.

The Celts imported some of these ornaments of silver and gold, as well as glassware and wine. In exchange, they traded tin from the Cornish mines, as well as iron, gold, and silver. They were renowned for their dogs, even then. They also traded cattle and slaves (Hibbert 1992, 16).

They were Druids, members of a religion who performed their rites with mistletoe by moonlight. As part of their rituals, they offered up human sacrifices—slaves or poor people—and animals. In expectation of an afterlife, the Celts buried their dead with weapons and ornaments.

The Celts built hill forts with turf and stone ramparts. They went into battle with swords, shields and daggers, their naked bodies dyed blue with woad (a dye made from a plant, Isatis tinctoria) and their long hair streaming in the wind. They drove their scythed chariots into battle and presented a terrifying sight to the Roman invaders. Caesar was impressed by their skill: ". . . by daily training and practice they attain such proficiency that even on a steep incline they are able to control the horses at full gallop, and to check and turn them in a moment. They can run along the chariot pole, stand on the yoke, and get back into the chariot as quick as lightning" (Churchill 1956, 16). A large area north of the Thames was ruled by Cassivellaunus, uncle of Shakespeare's Cymbeline, who was particularly successful in his attempts at resisting the Roman invasion.

Amazingly, the Celtic language survived the four hundred years of Roman occupation; in the other areas conquered by the Romans, this was not the case. In those regions the preexisting language was replaced by a Roman tongue and the Romance (or Roman) languages evolved— French, Italian, Portuguese, Romanian, and Spanish.

Gradually, as they retreated from various invaders, the Celts were driven westward, fleeing into Cornwall, and even over the Channel to Brittany (which means land of the Brits). They retreated into the mountains of Wales, over to the Isle of Man, to Ireland, and to Scotland. Their language survives as Scots Gaelic, Erse (or Irish), Welsh, Manx (spoken on the isle of Man), and Breton (Cornish died out in the eighteenth century) (Potter 1959, 18). In England the Celts left their mark on place names. Rivers include the Avon, the Cam, the Derwent, the Don, the Esk, the Ouse, the Severn, the Thames, Trent, and Wye. Names of towns include Bryn Mawr (meaning Great Hill), Carlisle, Dover, Leeds, and London. The word *Britain* is derived from the name of one group, the Prythons or Brythons. One of their tribes, the Cantii, gave their name to Kent and Canterbury, and another, the Dumnonii, gave theirs to Devon and Dorset. The prefix Mc/Mac, as in Mc/MacDonald, is Celtic. There are very few Celtic words in English, but they are the oldest in the language.

THE 3 ROMANS

Julius Caesar landed in Kent in 55 B.C.E. and returned the following year to capture Cassivellaunus's hill fort in Hertfordshire. After leaving Britain, he never went back, but in 43 C.E. (common era), Britain became a part of the Roman Empire under Claudius. The transition was not a smooth one, and the Celts resisted fiercely. A final rebellion was led by Queen Boadicea and the Iceni, a tribe of East Anglia. Enraged when their queen was mistreated by the Romans (she was flogged and her daughters raped), the tribesmen sacked the Roman town of Colchester and defeated the Ninth Legion which came to defend the town. They went on to burn the port of Londinium and to massacre the inhabitants. Rather than risk certain capture, Boadicea took poison. Eventually the country settled down to almost four hundred years of relative peace.

The Romans posted legions and built forts along the coasts and defended the north from incursions by building Hadrian's Wall, which the emperor Hadrian ordered built in 121 C.E. The wall, twenty feet high and over seventy-three miles long, with watch towers every mile, stretched across the width of England from the Tyne to the Solway, where you may still see it. The wall needed a garrison of fourteen thousand men, as well as five hundred to patrol it (Churchill 1956, 41). The Romans built towns with buildings of stone and slate, modeled on the Roman pattern with checkerboard streets and a central forum. They built temples, barracks, baths, and even amphitheaters. They crisscrossed the country with their straight metalled (built on a foundation of rock and stone) roads, and mileposts marking the distance to Rome. From Londinium, their capital, they built roads radiating out in all directions. Some of these roads are still in use.

They built baths, and centrally heated their beautifully furnished and decorated rooms. A visit to Bath, or to one of the many ruins of Roman villas, over six hundred of which have been excavated, gives an idea of the level of civilization attained by the wealthy. Particularly lovely are the mosaics in the Roman villa at Fishbourne in Sussex.

Despite their long occupation, the Romans left relatively little mark on the English language. Place names ending in *chester* (from Latin *castra* "camp") include Manchester, Winchester, Colchester, Dorchester, Leicester, Rochester, Westchester, and Chester itself; in most cases the Latin form was simply appended to a Celtic town name (Potter 1959, 19). The words that survived, an estimated 175 (Pyles and Algeo 1993, 287), were simple ones in everyday use, such as *mill, cook, kitchen, wine, cup, pound, cheap, inch, mile,* as well as *anchor* and *punt.* Words for vegetables and fruits that the Romans introduced—*beetroot, cherry, kale, mint, pea, peaches, pear, pepper, plum,* and *turnip*—also survived. The word *monger,* "trader," as in *ironmonger* or *fishmonger* is Roman (cf. modern *warmonger* and *scandalmonger*).

Most of the Latin words in our language do not date from this period, but were introduced by way of Norman French, as we shall see in a later chapter.

THE ANGLO-SAXONS

As the power of the Romans waned, Britain was attacked from all sides. From the north, the Pict warriors came back and overran Hadrian's Wall in 367 C.E. wiping out the legion in York. From the west, Irish pirates crossed the sea in small wooden and skin boats. But the largest group of invaders came from the Continent; they were the Angles, the Saxons, and the Jutes. They exterminated many of the Celts and drove the remainder into the hills of Scotland and Wales. Some fled to Brittany.

The Angles, after whom England was named, came from Schleswig (now Denmark and the land at the base of the Danish peninsula) and took their name from the angle of land that juts out into the southern Baltic Sea. The Jutes came from Jutland (now Denmark), the Saxons from Holstein (northern Germany below Denmark), and, a smaller group, the Frisians, from the islands off the coast of what is now Holland and Denmark. The Celtic inhabitants defended themselves as best they could. To make invasion more difficult, they narrowed the entrance gates to some of the cities. They appealed to Rome for reinforcements, but the Romans had troubles of their own. In 406 C.E. the Rhine river had frozen solid and thousands of barbarians had poured over the border into Roman territory. The Roman fleet that had previously guarded the British shores was no more, and the string of coastal forts established between the Solent and the Wash could no longer control the pirates. In 409 C.E. the last of the Roman legions left Britain.

In 446 the Celtic inhabitants sent a final appeal to Rome, and when that failed in 449 C.E., they even invited Saxon mercenaries, under the leadership of two chieftains, Hengest and Horsa (their names mean Horse and Stallion), to come to their aid, but the alliance was short-lived. These were turbulent times, and as no contemporary records survive, it is hard to know exactly what happened.

The Saxons, who got their name from the *seax*, the short sword they carried, were particularly bloodthirsty. As well as their swords, they carried iron-tipped spears, battle axes, and shields covered with hides. With their long flowing fair hair and beards they presented a fearsome appearance. They terrorized the inhabitants, pillaging, raping, and murdering. They burned and gutted the small Roman towns. Our main source for the history of these troubled times is the *Ecclesiastical History of the English Peoples* written in Latin by the Venerable Bede, about three hundred years later. He describes the misery of the times.

> None remained to bury those who had suffered a cruel death. A few wretched survivors captured in the hills were butchered wholesale, and others, desperate with hunger, came out and surrendered to the enemy for food, although they were doomed to lifelong slavery even if they escaped instant massacre. Some fled overseas in their misery; others clinging to their homeland, eked out a wretched and fearful existence among the mountains, forests, and crags, ever on the alert for danger. (Bede 1955, 13)

A record kept by the Church, the *Anglo-Saxon Chronicles*, provides other interesting details. Numbers to the left represent years.

410 Here the Goths destroyed the stronghold of Rome, and afterwards the Romans never ruled in Britain.

412 Here the Romans assembled all the gold-hoards which were in Britain and hid some in the earth so that no one afterwards could find them, and took some with them into Gaul.

443 Here the Britons sent across the sea to Rome and asked for help against the Picts, but they had none there because they were campaigning against Attila, king of the Huns; and then they sent to the Angles and made the same request.

At first, the invading Angles, Saxons, and Jutes returned to the Continent, but gradually, attracted by the fertile soil, they began to settle throughout England and brought their families across the sea in open boats. They were talented farmers, and with their iron axes and deep plows drawn by oxen were able to begin clearing the forests and cultivate the heavy clay soils of the midlands. They established the kingdoms of South Saxons (Sussex), East Saxons (Essex), and West Saxons (Wessex). It is to this period that the Celtic King Arthur belongs, and for about fifty years the invaders were kept out of Cornwall and the West Country.

In the north, the Angles settled and established themselves in what eventually became two kingdoms divided by the river Humber, whence the names, Northumbria and Southumbria or Mercia. Mercia adjoined Wales; the word is derived from marches "boundaries." The Jutes settled in Kent, Norfolk ('north folk'), and Suffolk ('south folk').

There were four Old English dialects: Kentish, West Saxon, Mercian, and Northumbrian. There were seven kingdoms: Northumbria, Mercia, East Anglia, Kent, Wessex, Sussex, and Essex. At the beginning of the ninth century Egbert (reigned 802-39), King of the West Saxons, took control of all seven kingdoms in a loosely bound confederacy.

Eventually Christianity became a force unifying and stabilizing this loose conglomeration. In 529 C.E. Benedict of Nursia had established the Benedictine Order at the monastery of Monte Cassino in southern Italy. The Benedictine monasteries spread and became influential centers of learning and industry. In 595 Pope Gregory I is said to have seen some fair-haired slaves in the market in Rome. When he inquired, he was told they were Angles. He replied, "non angli sed angeli" ('not Angles but angels') (Bryant 1953, 77). He sent St. Augustine, a Benedictine monk, with forty monks to convert Britain to Christianity. In 597 Augustine landed at Thanet, in Kent. The poet James Elroy Flecker imagines them walking over the Downs:

> I saw them march from Dover, long ago,
> With a silver cross before them, singing low,
> Monks of Rome from their home where the blue
>   seas break in foam,
> Augustine with his feet of snow...
>   "The Dying Patriot"
>   (The Home Book of Modern Verse p. 592)

Augustine succeeded in converting the Kentish King, Aethelbert, despite the latter's initial misgivings —he received them "sitting at his tent door lest they should cast spells on him" (Bryant 1953, 78). The king then used his influence to support Augustine and his monks. Augustine founded a monastery and a church in Canterbury and himself became the first Archbishop of Canterbury.

Over the course of the next two hundred years, these Benedictine monasteries became centers of learning, especially in the north. Knowledge and manuscripts went back and forth from Rome.

Hilda, Abbess of Whitby, was of royal descent, related to the King of Northumbria and a famous scholar. She founded a monastery at Whitby. One of the earliest Anglo-Saxon writings in the language is the hymn of Caedmon. Caedmon was a shepherd who dreamed of being commanded by a stranger to sing of all created things. When he awoke, he remembered the verses he had composed and wrote others. He was taken to the abbess, who realized that his gift came from heaven. He joined the monastery and continued to compose poetry.

The Venerable Bede, a Northumbrian monk, enjoyed the support of Benedict Biscop, who founded the Wearmouth-Jarrow monastery. A remarkable scholar, Bede adapted the Gregorian calendar, dating events from the birth of Christ. In his Ecclesiastical History he chronicled the history of the English nation. He also wrote a commentary on the Gospels and did some translation. He was indefatigable to the end. As he lay dying, dictating his final sentences, he cried out, "Write quickly; I know not how long I shall hold out." (Bryant 1953, 90)

In the monastery of Lindisfarne located on Holy Isle, off the coast of Northumbria, the monks produced glorious manuscripts. One of these, the Lindisfarne Gospel, miraculously survived devastation in the hands of the Vikings.

In 1939 a seventh-century royal burial ship was unearthed from the sands at Sutton Hoo in East Anglia. In the middle of a forty-oar open ship was a wooden burial chamber, filled with a treasure trove of silverplate, gold, jewelry, coins, weapons, armor, and other equipment. Preserved in the British Museum, the treasure attests to the skill of the Anglo-Saxon craftsmen (Green 1988, 97-101).

But the light of learning that burned so brightly, especially in the north of England, was to be extinguished by the next wave of invaders, the Danes. Here Bede describes the country that attracted these incursions (Bede 1955, 37-8).

> Britain is rich in grain and timber; it has good pasturage for cattle and draught animals, and vines are cultivated in various localities. There are many land and sea birds of various species, and it is well known for its plentiful springs and rivers abounding in fish. There are salmon and eel fisheries, while seals, dolphins, and sometimes whales are caught. . . . The country has both salt and hot springs, and the waters flowing from them provide hot baths, in which the people bathe separately according to age and sex. . . . The land has rich veins of many metals, including copper, iron, lead, and silver.

THE 5 DANES

Next to arrive were the Vikings. Strictly speaking, this term was applied to the Scandinavians engaged in piracy, but Vikings is the term by which they are best known. In Britain, although they came from what is now Norway, Sweden, and Denmark, they were collectively known as the Danes.

They were brave and energetic, but aggressive, incredibly cruel, and utterly relentless. They valued above all courage, loyalty, and generosity. Their younger sons, landless, since everything went to the eldest son, voyaged fortune-hunting all over the seacoasts of western Europe, and westward to Iceland and the New World. They built magnificent ships with dragon-headed prows and striped sails. The most famous of them, discovered in 1880, measured 76 feet 6 inches from stem to stern, was 17 feet 6 inches wide, but drew only 2 feet 9 inches amidships. It could carry a crew of fifty, as well as another thirty or so warriors or captives, for a month. And this was a ship of medium size (Churchill 1956, 92-3).

Throughout England, a chain of hilltop beacon fires was lighted by the inhabitants to warn of the raiders' coming. Initially, the Danes sailed their shallow-drafted ships up the rivers to conduct a series of attacks, pillaging, plundering, murdering, and then leaving. Sometimes they could be bought off with ransom money, known as *danegeld*, but then they would be back the next year wanting more. In 793 they sacked the monastery at Lindisfarne, and in 794 Bede's own monastery at Jarrow, fifty miles down the coast. They also pillaged the monasteries of Ireland. In 850 they sailed up the Thames with 350 ships. Finally, the only Saxon kingdom left with the strength to resist them was Wessex.

In 871 Alfred, the son of Æthelwulf, king of the West Saxons, came to the throne. He reigned for 28 years (d. 899) and became known as Alfred the Great. He fought the Danes valiantly and defeated them at Ashdown in the Berkshires, but then he was forced into hiding. According to a legend, a farm woman, not recognizing him, asked him to mind her cakes, and scolded him roundly because he let them burn.

Later, in 878, Alfred was able to rally sufficient support to defeat the Danes in a battle in the chalk hills near what is now Eddington. The white horse cut into the hillside at Bratton may have been made to celebrate that victory. Eight years later, Alfred forced the Danes into a treaty that kept them in an area north of a line drawn from London to Chester: Danes or Danelaw to the north, and Saxons to the south. Still today, this line marks a boundary between the speech of northern and southern England. If you travel northward into Yorkshire and the Lake District, you may find rural speakers difficult to understand. Alfred also built up a strong navy to discourage further incursions. Throughout the country he fortified towns or burghs (later known as boroughs) located in strategic sites and garrisoned by fighting men.

Thus many would-be Viking invaders were forced to settle elsewhere and some went to France instead. Hrolf der Ganger, or Rollo the Rover, their leader, made a treaty with Charles the Simple, one of Charlemagne's descendants. He agreed not to sail up the Seine and ravage Paris in exchange for being granted Normandy ('north man's land'). One of his descendants, William was to play a crucial role in the history of our language.

A scholar as well as a warrior, King Alfred set out to establish literacy among the freemen and the clergy, to train artisans, and to reestablish the monasteries. He spent nearly half of his revenue on education. He mastered Latin and translated into the vernacular Bede's *Ecclesiastical History*, St. Augustine's *Soliloquies*, Boethius's *Consolation of Philosophy* and other works. He encouraged the compiling of the first history of the English people in their own language. This *Anglo-Saxon Chronicle* continued to be kept for over two hundred years after his death and is a valuable source for the early history of the country. Alfred has been called the Father of English Prose. While uniting

England, he established English as an important language. No other English king is known as the Great. Think of him in the spring when the best of the early daffodils, King Alfreds, are in bloom.

The Danes spoke a North Germanic language, Norse, distantly related to the West Germanic of the Angles, Saxons, Jutes, and Frisians, who had driven out the Romans. Thus the two peoples could communicate to a degree. The Anglo-Saxon and Norse elements became so intermingled that linguists cannot always tell in which language a given word had its origin. In Yorkshire and up into Scotland, the Norse legacy is particularly strong. In that region over 1400 place names are Norse. The most common suffix *-by* meant village, as in Derby, Appleby, and Whitby; *gate* meant a street, as in Billingsgate; *thwaite*, a clearing, as in Crossthwaite and Braithwaite; *fell*, a hill, as in Scarfell; *beck*, a stream, as in Birkbeck, Caldbeck, and Troutbeck; *toft*, a piece of land, as in Lowestoft. Several days of the week are named for Germanic gods: Tuesday for *Tiew*, Wednesday for *Wodan*, and Thursday for *Thor*. *Egg* in the sense of *egg on*, *fro* in *to and fro*, and *red* as in *red up* ('to tidy up') are Norse (Potter 1959, 30). Sometimes Saxon and Norse forms survive side by side as follows:

Saxon	Norse
break	*breach*
craft	*skill*
ditch	*dike*
no	*nay*

raise	*rear*
shatter	*scatter*
shirt	*skirt*
whole	*hale*

(Bryson 1990, 53)

Many words beginning with the sound /sk/ are Norse, e.g., *scab*, *scold*, *scope*, *score*, *scrap*, *scree*, *scuff*, *skill*, *skin*, *skulk*, *sky*, and, of course, *ski*.

Common words of Norse origin include *awkward*, *bull*, *flat*, *happy*, *husband*, *law*, *meek*, *reef* (the nautical term), *root*, *rotten*, *sail*, *take*, and *ugly*. Verbs ending in *-en* are Norse, e.g., *happen*, *liken*, and *weaken*. Some verbs ending in *-le* are Norse, e.g., *dangle*, *dazzle*, *drizzle*, and *kindle*. Anglo-Saxon could not distinguish between *he* and *they*; just as we have difficulty with *you* and resort to "you all." Accordingly, the Anglo-Saxons adopted the Norse pronouns which became *they*, *them*, and *their*.

The Norse counted by 12s—a more convenient number than ten if you think of having to trade or divide property, for you can divide it into halves, quarters, thirds or sixths; 120 was a long hundred and is still known as such in some rural places. Until recently, British currency had twelve pence to a shilling, and we still buy eggs by the dozen.

King Alfred's successors were less successful than he at keeping the Norse invaders at bay. Particularly disastrous was the reign of Æthelred the Unready ('unwise'), which lasted from 978 to 1016. His life started with an evil omen; he fouled the baptismal font. Weak, impulsive, and cruel, he was incapable of governing. The Danes returned, and even those who had settled in the north returned to plundering. They demanded increasing sums of danegeld, which had to be extracted from the populace in the form of burdensome taxes. In 1002 AEthelred unwisely massacred the Danes at York, bringing down a terrible revenge at the hands of their leader, Sweyn Forkbeard. Finally, AEthelred fled to Normandy, leaving the country in the hands of Sweyn.

The Witan or Witenagemot ('meeting of wise men'), was a council of advisors to the Anglo-Saxon kings. In 1016 the Witan elected as their king a Dane, Canute, thereby uniting England, Denmark, and Norway into a single kingdom. A wise and strong ruler, Canute had been baptized and was devoutly Christian. Unfortunately he died in 1035 at the age of 40, leaving his sons to divide his kingdom among them.

The Witan's next choice was Edward, the son of AEthelred the Unready. Because of his piety, he became known as Edward the Confessor; so devout was he that he declined to provide an heir. His chief concern was the building of West Minster, on the bank of the Thames, and he neglected affairs of state. In 1161 he was canonized by Pope Alexander III and his shrine at Westminster became a center of pilgrimage (Churchill 1956, 149)

When Edward died in 1066, there were four contenders for the throne: the King of Norway,

Harald Hardraga; William, the Duke of Normandy; and two brothers of Edith, Edward's queen—Tostig, the deposed Duke of Northumbria, and Harold Godwinson. On the very day Edward was buried, in January 1066, Harold Godwinson had himself crowned in the newly built Westminster Abbey. His coronation was marked by the appearance of a "hairy star," actually Halley's comet, that was later interpreted to have been an ill omen.

OLD ENGLISH: THE LANGUAGE

Although, as we mentioned earlier, the Roman language had little influence on the Celts, the Anglo-Saxons adapted the Roman alphabet, which the Romans had themselves adapted from the Greek alphabet.

They added runic signs: æ as in *man* or *care*, ð and þ used interchangeably for *th*, ƿ the runic sign for *w*, and in early writing, œ later to become the German umlauted *ö* and the Scandinavian *ø* (Pyles and Algeo 1993 p. 49). There were no *j*, *q*, *v*, or *k*, and *z* occurred rarely; *y* was used for a vowel sound like the French *u* in *tu*.

Anglo-Saxon was a highly inflected language, rather like modern German. Nouns had number (singular and plural), gender (masculine, feminine, and neuter), case (nominative, genitive, dative, and accusative) and were inflected accordingly, as were the articles, pronouns, and adjectives that modified or agreed with them. Verbs were conjugated with inflectional endings that changed with each person and tended to be strong; that is to say, the vowels changed with the tense, as in English *take/took*, *drink/drank*, and *speak/spoke*. Then as now, English lent itself to compound words: astronomy was *tungolcraeft* or star-craft, an astronomer was *tungol-witega* or star-prophet, and arithmetic was *rimcraeft*, or number-craft (Potter 1959, 25).

Extant Anglo-Saxon texts include translations of the *Gospels*, Alfred's *Chronicles* and other works, and some poetry, of which *Beowulf* is the longest piece. The oldest is Caedmon's hymn. Some magnificent verse, well worth reading in translation, are "The Wanderer" and "The Seafarer," on similar themes. "The Dream of the Rood," inspired by the finding of a piece of the true cross, is a poem in the form of a riddle: first the poet describes what he sees, and then the cross speaks to him and tells its story. The "Battle of Maldon" is a magnificent short, almost Homeric, account of an encounter between the Saxons and the Danes. Also extant are gnomic verses, riddles, and charms. Here, in translation, is a short riddle (Alexander 1975, 100):

> The wave, over the wave, a weird thing I saw,
> Thorough-wrought, and wonderfully ornate:
> A wonder on the wave—water became bone.*

The following selection from the Gospel in Old English, the Annunciation scene, is readable because the text may be familiar:

---

*Answer: ice.

So þlice on þam syxtan monðe wæs asend Gabriel se engel fram drihtne

Thus on the sixth month was sent Gabriel the angel from God to

on galilea ceastre, Þære nama wæs nazareth, to beweddudre faemnan

a city of Gallilee, whose name was Nazareth, to a betrothed woman to

anum were, Þæs nam wæs iosep of dauides huse and þære faemnan

a man, whose name was Joseph of David's house and the woman's

nama waes maria. ða cwæ þse engel ingangende. Hal wes þu

name was Mary. Then quoth the angel going in unto her, "Hail be thou

mid gyfe gefylled: drihtgen mid þe: ðu eart geblestud on wifum.

with grace filled: the lord is with thee: Thou art blessed among women.

And a version of the Lord's Prayer (Chickering 1977):

Faeder ure,
our Father
þu þe eart on heofonum
thou that art in heaven
se þin nama gehalgod.
be thy name blessed
Tobecume þin rice
may become thy kingdom
Gewur þe ðin willa on eorðan swa swa on heofonum.
Be done thy will on earth as in heaven.

Urne gedæghwamlican hlf syle us to dæg.
Our daily loaf give us today.
And forgyf us ure gyltas, swa swa we forgyfad
    urum gyltendum.
And forgive us our sins, as we forgive others' sins.
And ne gelæd þu us on costnunge,
And do not lead us into temptation,
ac alys us of yfele. Soþlice.
but release us from evil. So be it.

The text that follows is from *Beowulf*. I have included the original text as well as a translation to give
some idea of the verse form. Each line was divided in
half and contained four beats, or stressed syllables. The
first stressed syllable in the second half-line established
the pattern of alliteration. One of the stresses in the
first half-line alliterated with it, and the other one
could. The last beat in the line never did. The verses
would have been sung by a scop, or minstrel, who
probably accompanied himself on a harp.

This passage describes the creation, as sung in
Beowulf's hall—a Christian element that was perhaps
a later addition to the pagan epic (Chickering 1977
lines 90-98):

Saegde, se þe cuþe
He spoke, who could tell
frumscreaft fira   feorran reccan
the beginnings of men   *knew their ancient origins*
cwæð þæt se Ælmihtiga   eorðan worhte
told how the Almighty   *had made the earth*
wlite-beorhtne wang   swa wæter bebugeð
this bright shining plain   *which the waters surround*

gesette sige-hreþig	sunnan ond monan
He victory-creative	*set out the brightness*
leoman to leohte	land-buendum
of sun and moon	*as lamps for earth-dwellers*
ond gefrætwade	foldan sceatas
adorned the green fields,	*the earth with branches*
leomum ond leafum	lif eac gesceop
shoots and green leaves	*and life he created*
cynna gehwylcum	þara ðe cwice hwyrfaþ
in each of the species	*which live and move.*

Beowulf contains passages of magnificent poetry, worthy of Homer. The new verse translation by Seamus Heaney promises to make the poem available to a wider audience.

The following is a description of Grendel's mere (Heaney 2000 lines 1362-76):

A few miles from here
a frost-stiffened wood waits and keeps watch
above a mere; the overhanging bank
is a maze of tree-roots mirrored in its surface.
At night there, something uncanny happens:
the water burns. And the mere bottom
has never been sounded by the sons of men.
On its bank, the heather-stepper halts:
The hart in flight from pursuing hounds
will turn to face them with firm-set horns
and die in the wood rather than dive
beneath its surface. That is no good place.
When wind blows up and stormy weather
makes clouds scud and the skies weep,
out of its depths a dirty surge
is pitched towards the heavens.

THE N7RMANS

The one date the English always know is 1066, that of the Norman Conquest. It is an important date for linguists as well as historians: it marks the beginning of the transition from Old English to Middle English. Certainly, no other single event had a greater impact on our language. It is therefore worth examining the unfolding of this momentous event in some detail.

The Normans were originally Vikings. They had settled in Normandy early in the tenth century, and in the intervening years had exchanged Norse language and barbarous ways for the language and manners of feudal France. By the treaty their original leader Rollo had made with the French king, Charles the Simple, the boundaries of the Duchy of Normandy were established. The Norman invasion of England was inspired by a desire to claim a throne they believed was rightfully theirs. William the Conqueror, as he came to be called, was their leader. His origin is fascinating, as Churchill (p. 153) tells it:

One morning, Duke Robert of Normandy, the fourth descendant of Rollo, was riding towards his capital town, Falaise, when he saw Arlette, daughter of a tanner, washing linen in a stream. His love was instantly fired. He carried her to his castle, and, although already married to a lady of quality, lived with her for the rest of his days. To this romantic but irregular union there was born in 1025 a son, William, afterwards famous.

William grew up to be Duke of Normandy and believed he had been promised the English throne. Outraged by the coronation of Harold Godwinson, he set about gathering the forces and ships necessary to mount an invasion. He enlisted the support of the pope, who dispatched a papal banner to inspire William's forces (Baker 1966, 99). By summer he was ready. He mustered his forces at the mouth of the River Dives and waited for a favorable wind. But the wind continued from the north for six whole weeks.

Meanwhile, on the opposing shore, Harold mustered his troops to await the Norman invasion. But as the unfavorable northerly wind continued, both sides had difficulty holding on to their troops who wanted to go home in time for the harvests.

As it happened, another event of consequence was also brewing. Only thirty years had passed since the rule of Canute, and the Norwegians decided to renew their rule of England and began to organize an expeditionary force under their king Harald Hardraga. They were joined by Tostig, Harold's exiled half brother. With a huge fleet, they sailed first to the Orkneys, where they added to their forces, and then, taking advantage of the same northerly wind that left William stranded, they moved down the coast to Yorkshire. They landed and headed for York.

As soon as he received the news, Harold marched north from Hastings where he had been preparing to meet the Normans. He was able to take the Norwegian invaders by surprise and rout them completely. Both Hardraga and Tostig perished in the Battle of Stamford Bridge.

Two days later the wind changed, and William and the Norman army set sail in more than a thousand ships and boats. They landed in Pevensey Bay and met with no resistance. William had time, actually two weeks, to build a fortification of earth and timber in the little port of Hastings and secure his bridgehead.

It took two days for the news of William's landing to reach York, where Harold was still celebrating his victory. Harold and his men set out immediately and covered the 190 miles to London in six days. There they waited for reinforcements, and early on the morning of October 12 they set forth, covering the 58 miles to Hastings in just two days. Early on October 14 the Normans set out to meet them. Their army of seven to ten thousand men was led into battle under the papal banner. Archers with bows and crossbows, men at arms, and mounted armored knights followed. Harold was still waiting for his army to arrive; he himself had ridden all night. His forces were tired and relatively ill equipped. The battle began at nine o'clock on the morning of October 14. The English fought valiantly and went on fighting even when there was no hope of victory, in the long tradition expressed in "The Battle of Maldon" (Alexander 1975, 123):

> Courage shall grow keener, clearer the will
> the heart fiercer, as our force faileth.

At twilight Harold fell, hacked to pieces by the Norman knights, one of whom cut off his leg (Hibbert 1992, 39), and surrounded by his dead thanes (freemen granted land in exchange for military service) and house-carls (body guards).

On Christmas Day William was crowned in Westminster Abbey, and a new era began. William lost no time in setting up a feudal system, confiscating lands and parceling them out to his followers (the usual way of rewarding a knight for his services was with a land grant), so that by the end of his reign there were only two English landholders left. He united the country by making service to the crown a condition of land tenure. He abolished serfdom; at the time of the Norman conquest there were over 25 thousand serfs (Baker 1966, 157). He established the jury system. By encouraging Jews to immigrate, he fostered trade and commerce. He was ruthless and brutal in crushing any rebellion, and by maintaining a strong army discouraged incursions from abroad.

One of William's first acts was to begin work on the *Domesday Book*, in which were meticulously recorded the ownership and value of everything that could be taxed. Included in the census were numbers of freemen, villeins, fields, mills, fish ponds, and plough teams—all recorded on long parchment rolls stored in the Treasury at Winchester. Eventually the documents were copied into two volumes, named the *Domesday* because, like Judgment Day, there was no appeal against it. In 1085 the recorder of the *Anglo-Saxon Chronicle* cannot suppress his shock at the thoroughness of the tax survey (Swanton, 216):

> . . . he had it recorded how much land his arch-bishops had, and diocesan bishops, and his abbots and his earls, and—though I tell it at too great length, what or how much each man had who was occupying land here in England, in land or in livestock, and how much money it was worth. He had it investigated so very narrowly that there was not one single hide [an old English measure of land, usually the amount that would support a single family], not one yard of land, nor even (it is shameful to tell—but it seemed no shame to him to do it) one ox, not one cow, not one pig was left out, that was not set down in his record.

By the time of the *Domesday Book*, the population of England was two million.

The Normans were great builders. They erected 500 castles within a generation of their arrival. These included the beginnings of Windsor Castle and the

Tower of London. They built cathedrals. Work on Durham Cathedral was begun in 1093, and by then fourteen major cathedrals were under construction. The rest were begun within the next hundred years, except Salisbury Cathedral, begun in 1220.

As well as their feudal system, the Normans brought with them their laws, their code of chivalry and knightly conduct, their hunting and falconry, their cooking and fashion, their architecture, and all the words connected with these.

For the next 300 years, no English king used English. In 1348 Edward III was dancing with Joan, the Duchess of Salisbury, when she dropped her garter. As he picked it up he said, "Honi soit qui mal y pense," ('Shamed be he who thinks evil of it') pronouncing the words that became the motto of the Order of the Garter. The king could speak English, but didn't in conversation (Hibbert 1992, 83). Thus the motto of the Order of the Garter remains French, as is that of the royal coat of arms "Dieu et mon droit" ('God and my right').

Under Edward III, England further increased her possessions, taking over a large portion of south-western France. In 1415 Henry V fought the battle of Agincourt and took possession of most of northern France. Not until the end of the Hundred Years War (1337-1453) and Joan of Arc were the English driven out of France. Calais, the last outpost, was not surrendered until 1558.

The Norman conquest and subsequent occupation were brutal events. Yet, the contribution of the Normans cannot be overestimated. Hilaire Belloc eulogized them as follows (*The Oxford book of English Prose*, 1035-7),

> The little bullet-headed men, vivacious, and splendidly brave, we know that they awoke all Europe, that they first provided settled financial systems and settled governments of land that everywhere . . . they were like steel when other Christians were like wood or like lead.

Churchill points out that the conquest "linked the history of England anew to Europe" (Churchill 1956, 176).

The two peoples, Saxons and Normans, intermarried and became so intermingled that a couple of hundred years after the Norman Conquest, it was no longer possible to tell them apart. They had become English.

8
MIDDLE ENGLISH

Throughout the period between 1066 and 1558 there was a great deal of interaction between the two countries. As a result, more than ten thousand words came into the language from Norman French (Balmuth 1992, 96), and most of them are still in use. Some words went back and forth across the Channel more than once: we cannot always tell who borrowed what from whom. Because French is a Roman, or Romance language, most of these words were Latin derived. Words connected with government include *country*, *duke* and *duchess*, *liege*, *parliament*, *prince*, and *sovereign* (but not *king* and *queen*, which are from Old English *cyning* and *cwen*), and the terms connected with heraldry. Military terms include *arms* and *armor*, *peace* and *war*, *battle*, *army* and *navy*, and the various ranks—*admiral*, *captain*, *lieutenant*, *officer*, *sergeant*, and *soldier*. The legal system gave rise to *court*, *judge*, *justice*, *jury*; to *attorney*, *defendant*, *plaintiff*; and to *felony*, *larceny*, and *petty* (as in petty theft). In addition to the word *religion* itself, imports included *angel*, *saint*, *savior*, *trinity*, and *virgin*, as well as *abbey*, *cloister*, *monastery,* and *relic*. The term *prie-dieu* is still in its original form. We probably recognize *gourmet*, *sauce*, *soup*, and *venison* as French words, but might not recognize *bacon*, *beef*, *veal*, *mutton*, *pork*, and *sausage* as being of French origin. The elegant court that eventually developed under the Norman French brought with it the words for gracious living: the words *leisure*, *art*, *architecture*, *ornament*, *design*, *costume*, *color*, and *paint*, as well as *joy* and *pleasure*, and *fruits* and *flowers*. The leisure class had time for sports—*falcon*, *quarry*, *scent*, and *chase*—and, in the evening they could play cards—*suit*, *trump*, *ace*, and *duce*—and gamble with *dice*.

During this period dating from 1100 to 1500, the English known later as Middle English was the language of the commoners and the uneducated. Thus the English language was able to develop in its own way, unchecked by any written form. It became simplified and inflexional endings were dropped. Gender became logical for nouns. If you have ever struggled with German, in which the word for *girl* is neuter (*das Mädchen*), *police* is feminine (*die Polizei*), *sun* is feminine (*die Sonne*), and *moon* masculine (*der Mond*), or with French, where *sun* is masculine (*le soleil*) and *moon* feminine (*la lune*), it is an improvement you can appreciate. Case endings and forms (complicated in Latin, and in present-day German and Russian) vanished except for pronouns, where they linger on, causing us to wonder about "it is me" versus "it is I," and the use of *who* versus *whom*. Plurals were formed increasingly by the addition of *s* or *es*, rather than through vowel change as in *man/men, mouse/mice* or *tooth/teeth*. The accent became fixed on the first or root syllable as the endings dropped off. Verbs became more regular; in the singular only the third-person final *s* remained. Strong verbs, such as *was/were, go/went, teach/taught* are today mercifully few in number—only 250 of them remain (Bryson 1990, 63). Only 4500 of these Old English words survive, less than one percent in a large dictionary, but they are the common ones we use daily.

During this transition period from Old English to Middle English, the southeast midland, Middlesex, became an important area for the development of language. It was the most densely populated area of England and included London, Oxford, and Cambridge. Additional fricative sounds developed. Old English had only /f/, /s/, /th/ (voiced and voiceless) and /sh/. New sounds: /v/ ,/z/, and /zh/ (as in leisure), and the diphthong /oy/, were added to the language. And so today we have *life/lives*, and *fox/vixen*. The Old English verb ending remained as the biblical *-eth* but elsewhere, under the influence of northern dialects, became modern *-s*; we say *gives, takes*, and *goes* rather than *giveth, taketh*, and *goeth*. Similarly the *-en* plural of *hosen*, and *shoen*, gave way to *-s* or *-es* except for *oxen* and *children*.

English eventually became the speech of the nobility, and by the end of the 1400s it had replaced

French in the courts, the Parliament, and the schools. Documents, titles, deeds, and wills were written in English. In 1362 the Statute of Pleading was enacted which required all court proceedings to be conducted in English. This was the period of Geoffrey Chaucer and the *Canterbury Tales*; Chaucer was probably twenty-two when the Statute of Pleading was enacted.

Geoffrey Chaucer (c. 1345-1400) lived through changing times and in a changing society. His lifetime spanned the reigns of three monarchs (Edward III, Richard II, and Henry IV). In the king's service, he traveled extensively to France, Spain, and Italy. He held important jobs that brought him into contact with a wide range of the populace: he was in service as a young page; served as a yeoman in the retinue of Prince Lionel in France (he was captured at the siege of Reims and had to be ransomed); served as an esquire in the royal household; was appointed Controller of the Customs of Hides, Skins, and Wools in the Port of London; was member of parliament for Kent; and was appointed Clerk of the King's Works (Chaucer 1992, xxviii-xxxvii). Important events in his lifetime included The Black Death, 1347-51, (which killed an estimated half of the population of England), the Peasant's Revolt, 1381, and the condemnation of John Wyclif, 1382 (who preached against the ecclesiastical hierarchy and wealth of the Church).

Because of his broad experiences, Chaucer was able to depict people from every walk of life. He began work on the *Canterbury Tales* while he was living in Kent, away from the Court, and worked on them again in the last years of his life. Unlike his other works, such as *Troilus and Criseyde* and *The Legend of Good Women*, which were aimed at a courtly audience, the *Canterbury Tales* was written for a wider group; furthermore, it was intended to be read by individuals, rather than to an audience. In his writings Chaucer used about eight thousand words, just over half of French or Latin origin (Potter 1959, 36).

Middle English, unlike old English, is comprehensible to modern readers, especially if they know French. It has been estimated that ten to fifteen percent of the words Chaucer used came from French (Pyles and Algeo 1993, 297). With a little practice and a glossary (the Everyman's Library version has notes and glossary on every page), you can learn to read Chaucer (?1343-1400) and the effort is worthwhile. The passage below is the well-known opening to the Prologue of *Canterbury Tales* (Chaucer, p. 1; my translation). Fourteen of the words in the passage are of French origin.

> Whan that Aprill with his shoures soote
> *When April with its sweet showers*
> The droghte of March hath perced to the roote,
> *Has soaked the roots, dry from the March drought,*
> And bathed every veyne in swich licour
> *And bathed every vein (sap vessel) in the moisture*
> Of which vertu engendered is the flour:
> *Which brings on the flower:*
> When Zephirus eek with his sweete breeth
> *When the west wind's sweet breath*

Inspired hath in every holt and heeth
Has inspired in every wood and field
The tendre croppes, and the yonge sonne
The tender crops, and the spring sun
Hath in the Ram his half course yronne,
Is half way through the Ram (Aries)
And smale foweles maken melodye
And small birds make melody,
That slepen al the nyght with open ye
That sleep all night with open eyes
Thanne longen folk to goon on pilgrimages.
Then folk long to go on pilgrimages.

And here is a less familiar passage, a description of the nun in the Prologue (Chaucer p. 4). Try to understand the lines before comparing the original with my literal translation that follows.

There was also a Nonne, a PRIORESSE,
That of hir smylyng was ful simple and coy;
Hire gretteste ooth was but by Seinte Loy;
And she was cleped madame Eglentyne.
Ful weel she soong the service dyvyne,
Entuned in hir nose ful semely,
And frenssh she spak ful faire and fetisly,
After the scole of Stratford atte Bowe,
For Frenssh of Parys was to hire unknowe.

. . . .

But, for to speken of hire conscience,
She was so charitable and so pitous
She wolde wepe, if that she saugh a mous
Kaught in a trappe, if it were deed or bledde.
Of smale houndes hadde she that she fedde
With rosted flessh, or milk and wastel-breed.

But soore wepte she if oon of hem were deed,
Or if men smoot it with a yerde smerte;
And al was conscience and tender herte.

There was also a nun, a prioress,
Whose smile was simple and modest:
Her strongest oath was but by Saint Loy;
And she was called madame Eglantine.
She sang the divine service very well,
Entoning the lovely notes through her nose,
And she spoke French elegantly,
With the accent learned at the school in Stratford-
    at-Bow,
For Parisian French was to her unknown.
But speaking of her sensitivity,
She was so charitable and full of pity
She would weep if she saw a mouse
Caught in a trap, whether it was dead or bleeding.
She had little dogs that she fed
With roast meat or milk and fine bread.
She wept bitterly if one of them was dead,
Or if men hit it smartly with a stick;
She was most sensitive and tender hearted.

Here is a somewhat later text, an extract from Sir
Thomas Malory's (?-1471) Morte d'Arthur. It was
printed in 1485 by William Caxton (c.1422-c.1491).
Malory describes the last meeting between Sir
Lancelot and Queen Guenevere (*The Oxford Book of
English Prose* 1925, 31). Can you decipher it?

So it was no bote ('use') to stryve, but he departed
and rode westerly, & there he sought a vij or viij

dayes, & atte last he cam to a nonnerye, & there was quene Guenever ware ('aware') of sir Launcelot as he walked in the cloystre. And whan she sawe hym there she swouned ('swooned') thryse, that all the ladyes and Ientyl wymmen had werke ynough to holde the quene up. So whan she myght speke she callyd ladyes & Ientyl wymmen to hir & sayd, Ye mervayl, fayr ladyes, why I make this fare ('affair'). Truly, she said, it is for the syght of yonder knyght that yender standeth. Wherfore, I praye you all, calle hym to me.

The language is well on its way to becoming the Modern English that we know.

THE CLASSICAL REVIVAL

As we mentioned, Latin and Greek contributed important elements to our language. The Classical Revival
was a period marked by renewed interest in the art,
architecture, and literature of Greece and Rome.

Athens had been at the height of its power from
about 460 to 421 B.C.E. Later Greek learning passed
into Latin (every educated Roman knew Greek) and
into Arabic, especially scientific texts on astronomy,
medicine, and mathematics. Eventually Arabic moved
west with the Moors into Europe by way of Sicily and
Spain. In 1453 the Turks captured Constantinople,
and Greek-speaking scholars fled to the west (Potter
1959, 139).

Some classical learning reached England with the
Church and the monastic tradition. The Venerable
Bede, in the eighth century, knew some Greek. Chaucer
knew only Latin. In the 13th century Roger Bacon and
in the 16th century Thomas More knew both Greek
and Latin. Thomas Linacre (c.1460-1524) traveled

widely in Italy and was one of the champions of classical learning. He served as physician to King Henry VII (whose son he tutored) and to Henry VIII. Erasmus of Rotterdam (1466-1536) taught Greek and Divinity at Cambridge, published the Greek text of the New Testament, and edited the works of St. Jerome. In later life he lived in Basel. He is said to have done more than any other man to advance the Revival of Learning.

Greek is relatively free of connotations, and Greek words are the more abstract elements of our language. When a name is needed for a new discovery or development, from *telephone*, *neon*, *nylon*, and *Xerox* (xero means dry), to *atom*, *proton*, *neutron*, and *cyclotron*, we turn to Greek. Greek words are readily compounded, e.g., *electrocardiogram* and *kleptomania*. Moreover, Greek has the advantage of being understood by scientists worldwide. Each term is exact and denotes only one thing, e.g., *carbon monoxide*.

Throughout the Classical Revival, English borrowed many Latin words in their original form: you can often recognize them by their endings: *-a*, *-um*, and *-us* in the singular, and in the plural *-ae*, *-a*, and *-i* respectively. These include *area*, *formula*, *insomnia*, *inertia*, *fulcrum*, *pendulum*, *momentum*, *maximum*, *minimum*, *nucleus*, *fungus*, *focus*, *genius*, *genus*, *ignoramus*, *radius*. About ten percent of the Latin words in English came directly from the Latin rather than through Norman French.

Sometimes scholars reintroduced a word that had already passed into English by way of Norman French, and both forms survived (much the same had happened with Norse and Anglo-Saxon).

Earlier Form	Scholar's Reintroduction
benison	*benediction*
chair	*chaise*
frail	*fragile*
poor	*pauper*

Sometimes scholars went back and amended the spelling to be in accord with the Latin. Parfit, as in Chaucer's "parfit gentil knyght" had been around for centuries (cf. ice cream parfait), but scholars changed the vowel and inserted the *c* to make it *perfect*, as in the Latin adjective *perfectus*. The earlier *avrille* was replaced by *April* to conform with Latin *aprilis*, and the pronunciation eventually followed suit. The *d* was inserted in *adventure*, and was pronounced. Spelling problems arose that still plague us, as scholars inserted the *b*'s in *February*, *debt*, and *doubt*, to conform with the Latin *Februarius*, *debitum*, and *dubitatum*.

While the classical influence was responsible for a vast influx of vocabulary and innumerable synonyms, this presented problems when the complexities were misused. E. B. White in *Elements of Style* (Strunk and White 1979, 23) quotes a Biblical passage George Orwell rewrote:

Objective consideration of contemporary phenomena compels the conclusion that success or failure in competitive activities exhibits no tendency to be commensurate with innate capacity, but that a considerable element of the unpredictable must inevitably be taken into account.

And contrasts it with the original King James version:

I returned, and saw under the sun, that the race is not to the swift, nor the battle to the strong, neither yet bread to the wise, nor yet riches to men of understanding, nor yet favor to men of skill; but time and chance happeneth to them all. (Ecclesiastes 9:11)

English and French words continue to exist side by side, but as Potter points out (Potter 1959, 37-38), generally the English words are the stronger, more physical, and more human. Compare *meet* with *encounter*, *heartfelt* with *cordial*, *lonely* with *solitary*, *friendship* with *amity*, *motherly* with *maternal*, *freedom* with *liberty*, *holiness* with *sanctity*, *depth* with *profundity*, and *happiness* with *felicity*.

The attempt to impose the structure and grammatical rules of classical language on English is misguided. Bryson writes (p. 137): "Making English grammar conform to Latin rules is like asking people to play baseball using the rules of football. It is a patent absurdity." Just because Julius Caesar didn't split infinitives (he couldn't have because the Latin infinitive is a single word!) or end sentences with prepositions is not reason enough for these rules. Split infinitives and sentences ending in prepositions come naturally to native speakers of English:

> Through wise investment we hope *to more than double* our income.
> Government has *to thoroughly investigate* the causes of urban poverty.
> They need *to carefully pick up* that broken glass.
> What on earth are you *up to*?
> Who did you borrow the money *from*?
> I don't care what he mixed it *with*.

TOWARD MODERN ENGLISH

10

Modern English, like Middle English, developed in the densely populated area that includes London, Oxford, and Cambridge. There is no sharp division between Middle English and Modern English as there was between Old English and Middle English. The Norman Conquest of 1066 had a sudden and far-reaching impact on the language. It is customary to consider, years from 1500 to 1650 as Early Modern English. The transition was a gradual one, with several influences and events at work; printing and the Great Vowel Shift were the first of these.

William Caxton (c. 1422-1491) was born in Kent but started in Bruges as a cloth merchant. He learned the art of printing in Cologne and in 1476 set up his wooden printing press in Westminster. He printed about a hundred books, including Chaucer's *Canterbury Tales* and Malory's *Morte d'Arthur*.

The Great Vowel Shift was another important influence on the development of the language. For reasons no scholar has fathomed, people started pronouncing vowels farther forward in the mouth, and existing front vowels were diphthongized. This change happened not all at once, but from about 1400 to 1600. Thus Chaucer's *lyf* (leef) became *life* and *hus* (hoos) became *house*. The next highest vowels moved forward to take their place. Chaucer's *ded* became *deed* and *mon* became *moon*. In addition, *e*, *o*, and *a* were lengthened, as in modern *break*, *home*, and *name*.

The northern, less populated, counties and the Irish were slower to make the changes: in Scotland, and even in the Lake District, one still hears *aboot* for *about*, *hoose* for *house*, and *path* and *bath*, as opposed to standard English *pahth* and *bahth*. Touring in Yorkshire a few years ago, I had car trouble, and was momentarily puzzled when the mechanic who came to my rescue said, "Flut buttery, eh?"

Unfortunately for those of us who have to teach the language, the Great Vowel Shift took place after spelling had been fixed by printing. The spelling never changed to reflect the new pronunciation, and English vowels have caused spelling problems ever since. There are about thirty vowel digraphs (two vowels together making a sound) in Modern English; most European languages have about four.

In many cases, the old pronunciation lingered on and accounts for some of the inconsistencies in the language (Fromkin and Rodman 1993, 455): *goose/gosling*, *sign/signal*, *sane/sanity*, *please/pleasant*, *crime/criminal*, *profane/profanity*.

At the beginning of Modern English, c.1500, fewer than 5 million spoke English: by 1700 there were twice as many speakers. During that period the language was further influenced by two literary monuments—The King James Version of the Bible and the work of Shakespeare.

In those years the entire population attended church. All the great houses had chapels, and even in the smaller ones morning prayer would be attended by all family members and servants. So it was that the glorious biblical prose seeped into the minds of the populace. The King James Bible or Authorized Version, published in 1611, was commissioned by the sovereign and composed by a panel of twenty-two of the leading scholars of the day. They proceeded from the original Hebrew and Greek texts, but relied heavily on an earlier translation, that of William Tyndale (1494 -1536). In fact, one third of the King James version is exactly as Tyndale wrote it. The scholars engaged to produce the King James version never acknowledged their indebtedness.

William Tyndale was born in Gloucestershire, close enough to the border to have developed an ear for the musical tones and rhythms of the Welsh language. He attended Magdalen College in Oxford, and then went on to Cambridge, where Erasmus had been teaching Greek. He was ordained a priest and hired by Sir John Walsh as tutor, a position which left him time to study the New Testament in Greek. Even then, he seems to have acquired some fame as a preacher.

The Bible in use in the churches at the time was the Latin Vulgate translated by St. Jerome (c. 340?-420) from Hebrew and Greek. The church fiercely resisted any attempts to translate the Bible into English and burned copies of English New Testaments together with their owners.

In this context Tyndale made his famous remark, as recorded by Foxe (1516-87), when a learned man said (Daniell 1994, viii): "We were better be without God's law than the Pope's": Master Tyndale hearing that, answered him, "I defy the Pope and all his laws, and said, if God spare my life ere many years, I will cause a boy that driveth a plough, shall know more of the scripture than thou dost."

Tyndale wanted to do his translating in London, but the bishop refused to give him the needed permission. About 1525 a wealthy merchant provided him with the necessary funds to travel to Germany. In Cologne, as he was overseeing the printing of the first New Testament in English, the print shop was raided, and he had to flee. In Worms his New Testament, translated into English from the original Greek, was published in 1526. Copies were hidden in bales of cloth and smuggled down the Rhine and across the Channel into English ports. In 1994 The British Museum bought the only extant copy for one million pounds.

Tyndale began to study Hebrew. In 1530 he published his translation of the first five books of the Old Testament, the first translation ever made directly from Hebrew into English. He felt that English was a better vehicle for the Hebrew original than was Latin (Daniell 1994, xxii): "And the properties of the Hebrew tongue agreeth a thousand times more with the English than with the Latin. The manner of speaking is both one; so that in a thousand places thou needest not but to translate it into the English, word for word." So remarkable was Tyndale's skill in Hebrew and Greek (and he knew six other languages) that even modern scholars consider his work sound.

In England the prelates continued to revile Tyndale, particularly Cardinal Thomas Wolsey. Even the otherwise reasonable Thomas More attacked him viciously and condemned him as a heretic who deserved to be burned. Eventually Tyndale was betrayed and imprisoned for sixteen months in a dungeon near Brussels; the influence of the English and papal authorities was strong in Belgium. On October 6, 1536, he was led out and tied to a stake, ceremoniously strangled in the presence of church officials, and burned. He was forty-two years old at his death.

A letter he wrote in Latin while he lay in the dungeon has been preserved (Daniell 1994, ix).

I suffer greatly from cold in the head, and am afflicted by a perpetual catarrh, which is much increased in this cell. . . .My overcoat is worn out; my shirts are also worn out. . . .And I ask to be allowed to have a lamp in the evening: it is indeed wearisome sitting alone in the dark. But most of all I beg and beseech your clemency to be urgent with the commissary, that he will kindly permit me to have my Hebrew Bible, Hebrew Grammar, and Hebrew Dictionary, that I may pass the time in study.

His pleas went unheeded and he was not able to write during his imprisonment.

The following passages, pure Tyndale, are virtually indistinguishable from the King James version:

Then God said: let there be light and there was light. And God saw the light that it was good: and divided the light from the darkness, and called the light day, and the darkness night; and so of the evening and morning was made the first day

(Genesis 1).

Now a passage from the New Testament:

And it fortuned while they were there, her time was come that she should be delivered. And she brought forth her first begotten son, and wrapped him in swaddling clothes, and laid him in a manger, because there was no room for them within in the inn. And there were in the same region shepherds abiding in the field and watching their flock by night . . .

(Luke 2)

Small wonder that the committee appointed by King James I could not improve on Tyndale's work, but resorted to "borrowing" unashamedly.

Thomas Cranmer's *Book of Common Prayer*, completed by the Archbishop of Canterbury in 1549 for the (non-Roman) Church of England, was an equally strong influence on the English language. Jonathan Swift (1667-1745) wrote (*The Oxford Book of English Prose* 1925, 339), "If it were not for the Bible and the Common Prayer Book in the vulgar Tongue, we should hardly be able to understand anything that was written among us an hundred years ago; which is certainly true; for those books, being perpetually read in Churches, have proved a kind of standard for language, especially to the common people."

The accomplishments of William Shakespeare (1564-1616) must be viewed with awe; he is rightly called the Immortal Bard. He wrote plays that were not simply acted, but also widely read. His impact on our language is incalculable. Hundreds of expressions that we use freely, we speak just as Shakespeare wrote them, often ignorant of the source (McCrum, Cran, and MacNeil 1992, 81):

in the mind's eye	a killing frost
parting is such sweet sorrow	hoist by his own petard
a plague on both your houses	white as driven snow
a rose by any other name	a pound of flesh
ill met by moonlight	like patience on a monument
my kingdom for a horse	the green eyed monster (jealousy)

ripeness is all	this rough magic
breathing one's last	backing a horse
a fool's paradise	too much of a good thing
into thin air	tongue-tied
seen better days	the more fool you
a tower of strength	more in sorrow than in anger
give the devil his due	truth will out

English has always had the capacity to make words serve as more than one part of speech. Thus we can use the word *fish* as a noun, a verb, or an adjective. Shakespeare engages in this practice freely (Potter 1959, 57):

> *Scarf up* the tender eye of day (noun as verb)
> ... strew me over
> With *maiden* flowers...(noun as adjective)
> Woulds't be *window'd* in great Rome? (noun as verb)
> That from their own misdeeds *askance* their eyes
>   (adverb as verb)

Shakespeare, like Tyndale, used the Anglo-Saxon words as the more familiar and direct. When he does slip in Latin multisyllabics, the effect is astounding:

> No, this my hand will rather
> the *multitudinous* seas *incarnadine*,
> Making the green one red.
> (Macbeth Act II Scene 2)

Shakespeare coined words freely. About 1700 of his creations have survived (Bryson 1990, 76, and

McCrum, Cran, and MacNeil 1992, 81): *barefaced, critical, castigate, countless, dislocate, dwindle, excellent, frugal, gust, hint, hurry, leapfrog, lonely, majestic, monumental, obscene, premeditated, submerged, summit.* He had a huge vocabulary, an estimated 30 thousand words—most of us command half as many (McCrum, Cran, and MacNeil 1992, 95).

We know very little about Shakespeare's life. He was born in Warwickshire, at Stratford-on-Avon, moved to London, and returned to his birthplace. He was familiar with the country speech of his region, but could and did write in the Welsh and Scots dialects (Henry V, IV.1 and V.1). He could write the common language for the audience in the pit, as in the following passage where Pistol, a soldier, expresses his admiration for his king all in words of one or two syllables (Henry V, IV. 1):

> The King's a bawcock, and a heart of gold,
> A lad of life, an imp of fame;
> Of parent's good, of fist most valiant.
> I kiss his dirty shoe, and from heart-string
> I love the lovely bully.

And he could speak the language of the court, interspersing longer words (Henry IV, Pt. I, I.2):

> I know you all and will awhile uphold
> The unyoked humor of your idleness:
> Yet herein will I imitate the sun,
> Who doth permit the base contagious clouds
> To smother up his beauty from the world

That when he please again to be himself,
Being wanted, he may be more wonder'd at
By breaking through the foul and ugly mists
Of vapors that did seem to strangle him.

Other English writers of less monumental stature were important because they were widely read: John Bunyan (1628-88), Daniel Defoe (1660-1731), and Jonathan Swift (1667-1745). Also influential were the journalists Joseph Addison (1672-1719), Richard Steele (1672-1729), and the satirical poet Alexander Pope (1688-1744).

For several centuries Bunyan's *Pilgrim's Progress* was a book found in many households. Bunyan, like Tyndale, lived in a time of religious intolerance and prosecution. But when the monarchy was overthrown and Oliver Cromwell came to power, the country enjoyed a period of relative religious tolerance. Bunyan joined the Baptist Church (he was baptized secretly at midnight—there were limits to religious freedom) and was able to preach. He believed and preached that prayer should be from the heart, rather than from a text. But in 1660 came the restoration of the monarchy under Charles II and the end of religious tolerance. Bunyan was arrested, and since he refused to stop preaching, he spent the next twelve years in prison. His imprisonment was hard on his family, especially as his oldest daughter had been born blind. Finally, in 1672 he was granted a license to preach.

Pilgrim's Progress, subtitled *In the Similitude of a Dream*, was composed during Bunyan's imprisonment. Much of it is dialogue, between the Pilgrim Christian, his guide, and the personifications of the various temptations that he meets as he wends his way in an allegorical journey towards salvation.

> Then Evangelist gave him a Parchment-roll on which were written the words, Fly from the wrath to come. The Man therefore read it and, looking at Evangelist very carefully, said, Whither must I fly? Then said Evangelist pointing with his finger over a very wide Field, Do you see yonder Wicket-gate? The Man said, No. Then said the other, Do you see yonder shining light? He said, I think I do. Then said Evangelist, "Keep that Light in your eye and go up directly thereto: so shalt thou see the Gate; at which when thou knockest, it shall be told thee what thou shalt do.
>
> (Harvard Classics 1909 vol.15, 15)

Bunyan uses long sentences; his syntax is often involved. Many common nouns are capitalized, as they still are in German.

Daniel Defoe, born the son of a butcher, wrote political pamphlets, one of which resulted in his imprisonment. *Robinson Crusoe*, published in 1719, enjoyed popular success and though written for adults, is still read by children. He also wrote *Moll Flanders* and *A Journal of the Plague Year*, and from 1711 to 1713 single-handedly produced a periodical, *The Review*. His prose is clearly modern:

It happened one day about noon, going towards my boat, I was exceedingly surprised with the print of a man's naked foot on the shore, which was very plain to be seen in the sand. I stood like one thunderstruck, or as if I had seen an apparition. I listened, I looked round me; I could hear nothing, nor see anything. I went up to a rising ground to look farther. I went up the shore and down the shore; but it was all one, I could see no other impression but that one.
(Swift 1932,153)

Jonathan Swift, born in Ireland, became the chief political writer of the Tory party. In 1714 he returned to Ireland and wrote a series of pamphlets, including A Modest Proposal, in which with bitter irony, he suggested that Ireland's problems could be helped by using the children of the poor as food for the rich. *Gulliver's Travels*, a piece of political satire, appeared in 1726. The following intricate sentences give some idea of his prose style.

My father had a small estate in Nottinghamshire; I was the third of five sons. He sent me to Emanuel college in Cambridge, at fourteen years old, where I resided three years, and applied myself close to my studies; but the charge of maintaining me, although I had a very scanty allowance, being too great for a narrow fortune, I was bound apprentice to Mr. James Bates, an eminent surgeon in London, with whom I continued four years; and my father now and then sending me small sums of money, I laid them out in learning navigation, and other parts of the mathematics, useful to those

who intend to travel, as I always believed it would
be, some time or other, my fortune to do.
(Swift 1931, 63)

Gullivers Travels was "the first full-length piece of
prose fiction written in the plain style of early
eighteenth-century expository prose with continuous
colloquial overtones. . ." (Daicher 1960, 600).

Sir Richard Steele was probably the first, but by
no means the last, to worry about preserving the
language and resisting change: "But what I have most
at Heart is, that some Method should be thought on
for ascertaining and fixing our language for ever. . . ."

Joseph Addison and Steele met while they were
still in school, attended Oxford together, and enjoyed
a long and fruitful literary friendship until political
disagreement led them to part ways. *The Tatler*, a
largely political journal, appeared in the years 1709-
11. Then they collaborated on *The Spectator*. Their
objective was to bring learning "out of closets and
libraries, schools and colleges, to dwell in clubs and
assemblies, at tea-tables and in coffee houses" (Daicher
1960 p. 545). No less an authority than the great Dr.
Johnson praised *The Spectator* as a model of prose
style: "Whoever wishes to attain an English style,
familiar but not coarse, and elegant but not
ostentatious, must give his days and nights to the
volumes of Addison" (Daicher 1960, 598). Over 3,000
copies of *The Spectator* were printed daily, and 555
numbers were collected into seven volumes; an eighth
volume was added in 1717.

Alexander Pope, born in London, suffered from poor health and curvature of the spine. His appearance made him an object of mockery. He was born a commoner and a Roman Catholic when titles were important and when Catholics were barred from universities and public office. Even in childhood he "developed a precocity so intense as to be ferocious" (Untermeyer 1942, 528). At the age of ten he translated Greek and Latin, and at twelve he wrote one of his best-known poems, "Solitude," that begins:

Happy the man, whose wish and care
A few paternal acres bound,
Content to breathe his native air
In his own ground.

He became known for his mastery of the heroic couplet—a ten-syllable line, usually in iambic pentameter. His biting satirical verse gained him enemies, but the precision and brilliance of his verse was undeniable. His best-known work was a mock epic, "The Rape of the Lock." It was based on an incident —considered scandalous—in which a certain Lord Petre surreptitiously cut a lock of hair from the head of Miss Arabella Fermor (Untermeyer 1942, 534). Some of Pope's lines are still quoted today:

A little learning is a dangerous thing
The proper study of mankind is man.
Hope springs eternal in the human breast.
Fools rush in where angels fear to tread.

Finally, two great dictionaries contributed immensely to our language. Dr. Samuel Johnson (1709-

84), a poet and a critic immortalized by his biographer, James Boswell, undertook the enormous task of compiling the language. He worked in a garret with a long desk running down the middle at which his six clerks could work. He gathered definitions for over 40,000 words and illustrated their meanings with over 114,000 quotations, compiled by reading through Shakespeare's works and everything subsequently written. He spent nine years on his compendium, which was finally published in1755 and remained the standard work through the nineteenth century. Some of his definitions became famous, e.g.:

> Lexicographer—A writer of dictionaries, a
> harmless drudge.
> Oats—A grain which in England is given to
> horses, but in Scotland supports the people.

Johnson was under no illusion that his dictionary would, or should, fix the language, or even stabilize the spelling. He wrote that no lexicographer should imagine that "his dictionary can embalm his language, and secure it from corruption and decay," and "sounds are too volatile and subtile for legal restraints; to enchain syllables and to leash the wind, are equally the undertakings of pride." English, unlike French, was never to have an Academy to keep it in line.

James Murray (1837-1915) took up work on the *Oxford English Dictionary* in 1878 and continued his efforts for the rest of his life. The dictionary, five decades in the making, was completed by others in 1927. Following the example of Johnson, Murray decided that each word should be illustrated with quotations from all that had been written. One of his first tasks was to enlist the help of readers in "Great Britain, America, and the British Colonies, to finish the volunteer work so enthusiastically commenced twenty years ago, by reading and extracting the books which still remain unexamined" (Winchester 1998, 113). Incredibly laborious as was the task of sorting and ordering the thousands of contributions that rolled in daily, there was no other way of discovering the various shades of meaning a word has passed through in its lifetime. Thousands of these definitions came from Dr. William Minor, an American graduate of Yale, imprisoned in England at Broadmore, an asylum for the criminally insane. The amazing story of his life and contributions has been told by Simon Winchester in *The Professor and the Madman.*

The April 10, 2000 Arts Section of the *The New York Times* featured an article about the *Oxford English Dictionary* titled "Staid Know-It-All goes Hip and Online." The current dictionary extends to twenty large volumes, is cumbersome to use, and once printed cannot be readily revised. The planned $55 million ten-year overhaul will add 600,000 new words and will be available on line to subscribing libraries and individuals. As well as making constant revision possible, the new online format will make the information more accessible. "The current editors aided by a world-wide network of volunteers, are consulting documents from the United States, Australia, and other English-speaking countries, and using non-literary works from the past and the present" (Lyell 2000 1; 6) The O.E.D.'s principal philologist, Edmund Weiner is quoted as follows. "One hundred years ago it wasn't respectable to put a lot of colloquial language and slang words into print. It's only been in the last century that the gap between written and spoken language has narrowed" (Lyell 2000 1; 6). The development of the online O.E.D. certainly promises to be a boon to scholars and readers in the new millennium.

AMERICAN ENGLISH 11

> Oh, paint your wagons with "Pike's Peak or Bust!"
> Pack up the fiddle, rosin up the bow,
> Vamoose, skedaddle, mosey, hit the grit!
> (We pick our words like nuggets for the shine,
> And where they didn't fit, we make them fit,
> Whittling a language out of birch and pine.)
>   Stephen Vincent Benet, Western Star

English no longer means "the king's English." There is one English language; the similarities between British and American English are far greater than the differences—despite George Bernard Shaw's ironic assertion that "England and America are two countries separated by the same language."

Not only did English evolve in the New World, but the language spoken in Britain also changed. George III would have pronounced *after*, *ask*, and *dance* as we Americans do today. Some words we think of as American actually represent older British usage, e.g., *gotten*, *fall* (for autumn), and *deck* rather than *pack* as in

Alice in Wonderland's *pack* of cards (Pyles and Algeo 1993, 212-13). In the mid-nineteenth century attempts were made in the state legislatures and in the congress to change the name of the language spoken in this country to "American language" or even to adopt another language—Hebrew and Greek were suggested as the official language of this country (Pei 1984, 326). H. L. Mencken quotes Thomas Jefferson as saying: "The New Circumstances under which we are placed call for new words, new phrases, and for the transfer of old words to new objects. An American dialect will therefore be formed (Mencken 1931, 1)." A dialect is perhaps correct, but not a new language as Mencken called it; he titled his book *The American Language*. It is amusing to note that in 1921 the university in Paris hired two new lecturers, a *lecteur d'anglais and a lecteur d'américain* (Mencken 1931, 27).

However, there are a number of differences between British and American English. The first is vocabulary. Words were added for new items (*caribou, locust, opossum, raccoon, tomahawk*), borrowed from other languages, especially from the French fur trappers and explorers (*bayou, cache, crevasse, levee, portage, prairie*), from the Spanish (*adobe, alligator, armadillo, canoe, canyon, castanet, coyote, mesa, vamoose* from *vamos* 'let's go'), and from the Dutch (*buoy, cookie, leak, sleigh, waffle, yacht*). Although words from native American languages (*hickory, hominy, papoose, squash, wampum*) numbered well over a hundred, place names were the greatest contribution from that source. These include: states, Alabama, Dakota, and Minnesota; four of the five Great Lakes; mountain ranges, Allegheny and Appalachian; and towns, Chicago and Sitka. Nearly half our place names are borrowed from native Indian languages (Fromkin and Rodman 1993, 461).

Much later, *elevator*, *truck*, *sneaker*, and *bobby pin* replaced the English *lift*, *lorry*, *pimsole*, and *kirby grip*. We tend to say *baggage* for *luggage*, *mailman* or *letter carrier* for *postman*, *package* for *parcel*, and *pocketbook* for *purse*. Since we are a nation of immigrants, the process of acquiring new words continues. World-War II brought *blitzkrieg*, *kaput*, and *kamikaze* from onetime enemies. *Peristoika* and *glasnost* came into the language from Russia during the Gorbachev era.

American English has a knack for coining new words by analogy. Thus *watergate* (originally a building) gave rise to *whitewatergate* and *travelgate*, and the suffix *gate* took on the meaning of something unethical. *Automat* started as a trade name for a food-vending machine, and led to *Laundromat*. Trade names such as *cellophane*, *escalator*, *Kleenex* and *Xerox* became generalized in meaning.

Shakespeare could confidently change a word from one part of speech to another, an easy feat in an uninflected language, and the process continues. We can *contact* our friends, arrange for a *get-together*, meet at the *drive-in*, see a *show*, and *party* all night. We can arrange for a *check-up*, *star* in a movie, and go *ape*.

Idioms, especially those concocted with get and fix continue to proliferate. We can *get around to it*, *get away with it, get back at, get back to, get even, get into, get off on, get on with it,* and *get over it.* We can speak of *fixing* a jury, *fixing* someone up with a date, *fixing* on a place, *fixing* a schedule, getting the cat *fixed*, and in the South *fixing* to sell the house—with widely divergent meanings. American English is rich in vivid idiomatic expressions, some of them rooted in the early history of our country, e.g., *pay dirt, fool's gold, bark up the wrong tree, up a creek without a paddle, a full head of steam, nickel and dime, a square deal, a cold fish, never darken his door.*

Pronunciation has changed too, and even television and radio have failed to eliminate the regional dialects. Ironically, through radio and television, and through troops stationed in England during World War II, both American vocabulary and pronunciation have spread back to the British Isles, and the differences between the two variants are increasingly blurred. There are greater differences between the speech of London and Glasgow than there are between London and New York. On the other hand, words such as *schedule, lieutenant, squirrel,* and *herb* continue to be pronounced differently. British English drops a syllable in words such as *library, preliminary, extraordinary, laboratory* and *military.* In most American speech long *u* is pronounced *oo* (as in *grew*) rather than *yoo* (as in *few*) in words such as *due, dual, neuron* and *neutral.* We tend to accent the first syllable in words like *adult, romance,* and *recess* (Mencken, 217).

Noah Webster, (1758-1843) author of *American Dictionary of the English Language* (1828) and of "Webster's Spelling Book" (1783) advocated simplified spelling. By 1889 sixty-two million copies of his spelling book had been sold; moreover, Mencken credits him with finally achieving "the divorce between English example and American practise" (1931, 236). Webster eliminated the *u* in words such as *color*, *favor*, and *neighbor*, and changed from *re* to *er* on the end of words such as *theater*, *center*, and *meter* (Pyles and Algeo 1993, 226). The British still write *cheque*, *gaol*, *pye* ('pie'), *pyjamas*, *traveller*, *tyre*, *waggon*, and *woollen*, but for most of these the American forms are also in use (Pyles and Algeo 1993, 226). In rural Pennsylvania, I have heard, "I knowed it" and "I seed it" and a paper bag is still a *poke* (as in a pig in a poke).

Black English is probably more a political issue that a real variant (Pyles and Algeo 1993). However, there are differences in pronunciation and grammar. For example: *ask* and *aunt* are pronounced *ax* and *ant*; in verbs the final *s* is often omitted (she love you), the *-ng* ending changed to *-in* (comin) and *be* substituted for *is* (he be working now) to denote ongoing action.

With the rise of the women's movement and the emphasis on non-sexist language, recent years have seen changes from *chairman* to *chairperson*, and finally to *chair*. The *mailman* has become a *letter carrier*; the *stewardess*, a *flight attendant*; and the *fisherman*, a *fisher*.

We tend to resist change, and correct our children about the difference between *can* and *may*, *who* and *whom, different from* versus *different than, between* and *among,* Purists among us resist the use of *hopefully* (as in *hopefully* tomorrow will be sunny), of the double negative (perfectly acceptable in Spanish—only in mathematics do two negatives make a positive), and object to the change in meaning that has overtaken *presently* (which used to mean in a while), and *momentarily* (which used to mean for a moment). I confess to some anxiety every time the flight attendant announces, "Our plane will take off momentarily." A living language is constantly changing, and we can no more turn back the tide than could Canute. As Pyles and Algeo state "Language is a living thing, our possession and servant rather than an ideal toward which we should all hopelessly aspire" (1993, 210). They earlier expressed the following intriguing notion, "Every language is constantly turning into something different, and when we hear a new word, or a new pronunciation or novel use of an old word, we may be catching the early stages of a change" (1993, 13)

Finally, in modern American, sentences became shorter and syntax less convoluted. The best of Mark Twain or Ernest Hemingway is worthy of Tyndale.

THE ROOTS OF
OUR LANGUAGE

And the whole earth was of one language and of one speech.

Genesis 11:1

So here we have our language: approximately fifty-five percent Latin, ten percent Greek, one percent Germanic (in any large dictionary), and the rest from innumerable other sources and unknown origins. But even more fascinating is the fact that these languages, Latin, Greek, and Germanic, were at one time one language, for they all had their origin in what we call Indo-European. Proto-Indo-European, the ancestor of so many languages, was never written, but scholars have been able to reconstruct much of it.

In the late eighteenth century William Jones, a British civil servant, was functioning as a judge in Calcutta. He spent his spare time teaching himself Sanskrit, the language of the ancient Hindu sacred texts. He was surprised to note that the language had much in common with Greek and Latin, with which he was familiar. There were obvious similarities. For instance:

devas/divine
rajas/ regal, royal, reign
sarpas/ serpent
trayas/ trinity
pitr/paternal, patronize

In 1786 Jones presented a paper to the Asiatick (sic) Society in Calcutta in which he concluded that the relationship between Latin, Greek, and Sanskrit was stronger "than could have possibly been produced by accident; so strong, indeed, that no philologer could examine them all three, without believing them to have sprung from some common source which, perhaps, no longer exists" (Claiborne 1989, 6).

The Indo-Europeans, as noted in Chapter 1, began to migrate about 3500-2500 B.C.E. taking their language with them. They eventually spread all over Europe, eastward to India, and far western China. As they moved, their language spread, and as it spread, it constantly changed.

Between 1822 and 1840 Jacob, one of the Brothers Grimm who collected the fairy tales, accomplished the incredible feat of formulating the laws that governed some of the changes. Named for him, one set of changes is known as Grimm's Law.

Indo-European had 18 consonants. In the shift to Germanic (but not to Latin or Greek), half of them changed. However, the liquid sounds, *l* and *r*, and the nasals, *m* and *n*, remained unchanged in all three languages. These changes took place over hundreds of years.

The first to change were the three unvoiced stops, which changed to fricatives, or breathed sounds. Thus:

p to f as in:
    pater/father
    penna/feather
    penta/five
    pisces/fish
    pod (as in tripod)/foot
    pyre/fire

t to th as in:
    mater/mother/
    pater/father
    tres/three
    tumor/ thigh, thumb (perceived as the swollen parts of the leg and hand respectively).

k to h as in: cornet/horn
    cardiac/heart
    canine/hound
    cannabis/hemp

This change left the language with no unvoiced stops, p, t, k, and eventually the voiced stops, b, d, g, shifted to replace the lost sounds. Thus:

b to p as in:
    reimburse/purse
    boast/ puff
    bosom/pouch, pocket

d to t as in:
    decade/ten
    dentist/tooth
    domestic/tame

g to k as in:
    agriculture/acre
    grain/corn
    grate/scratch
    genuflect/ knee

Sanskrit has three other sounds—as do Hindi and other Indian languages—*bh*, *dh*, and *gh*, which you may have noticed in Indian words such as *Bhagavad Gita*, *dharma*, *dhoti*, *ghat*, *ghee*, and other Indian words that we hesitate to pronounce. These sounds are simply voiced stops followed by a puff of air, and they shifted to replace the missing voiced stops.

This is an oversimplification. Other factors such as the position in the word and accent affected the changes too.

If you happen to know even a little German, you will have been struck by some interesting differences between English and German. The so-called second sound shift is responsible. This began in Bavaria, probably in the fifth century C.E., and moved slowly northward. It distinguishes German from English, Dutch, and the Scandinavian languages. Affected were the consonants that had changed under Grimm's law. A few examples follow (Chambers and Wilkie 1970, 112-13):

	English	**German**
p became f as in:	open	offen
	sleep	schlafen
	ship	Schiff
t became s as in:	water	Wasser
	eat	essen
	what	was
k became ch as in:	make	machen
	seek	suchen
	reek	rauchen
p became pf as in:	apple	Apfel
	pan	Pfanne
	pound	Pfund
d became t as in:	bid	bitten
	do	tun
	hand	hant
		(spelled Hand)

No explanation has been found as to why such changes occurred.

About 2000 Indo-European roots have been reconstructed. As mentioned earlier, eighty percent of English vocabulary is derived from Germanic, Latin, and Greek sources (Claiborne 1989, 5). Most of these words can be traced back to their Indo-European roots. Potter points out, "Of all the tongues descended from Indo-European, English has had the most contacts with its kindred near and far" (Potter 1959, 14). The following will give some idea of the richness of this heritage. The roots are asterisked because they are reconstructions (Claiborne is my source for the following).

*DEIW 'to shine,' also the shining sky and the sun, and because these early people were sun-worshipers, god

> *deity, divine, adieu, diurnal, diary, journal, Jove, dial, diet, adjourn, Zeus, Tiw* (as in Tuesday), dismal from the Latin *dies malus* "bad day"). In this instance the sound changes are such that the connection is difficult for a layman to make. However, it is worth noting that even in our speech /d/ changes to /j/ before a long *u*; pronounce the words *would you* rapidly, and you will observe the change.

*PA 'to protect'

> *feed, food, fodder, forage, foster, fur* (that which protects you), *pasture, pastor, repast, antipasto, pantry, companion, company, pabulum.* Here you can note the change from *p* to *f* that occurred with Grimm's Law.

*KERS 'to run,' and perhaps horse

> *course, current, corridor, career, cursor,* and in a figurative sense *concur, discourse, excursion, precursor,* and so forth and from another branch *cart, carriage, car, chariot, cargo, carpenter.*

*BHERGH 'high,' 'hill,' 'hill fort'

> *iceberg, belfry, borough, berg, burgher, burglar,* and innumerable town names ending in -*burg*, -*burgh*, or -*borough*.

*BHEDH 'to dig'

> the fossils that are dug up, the soft ground that has been dug up, and the soft bed on which we sleep.

*UL 'to howl'

> *owl*

*WOPSA

> *wasp*

When you speak these words, you are using derivations of roots existing more than 5000 years ago. Half the population of the world speaks an Indo-European-descendant language.

APPENDIX
WHENCE THESE
WORDS?

An interesting form of dictionary practice is to have students try to guess the language of origin, look up the words in an unabridged dictionary to check their guesses, and perhaps explain the history behind the derivation.

The following lists can be used to initiate this activity.

Spanish	French
alligator	antique
avocado	beige
buffalo	chic
chocolate	chowder
coyote	gopher
hurricane	menu
lariat	parachute
mosquito	prairie
mustang	restaurant
sombrero	rouge

Some words in common use come from a variety of languages:

African: *banjo, jazz, gumbo, tote,*
American Indian: *moose, opossum, raccoon, wigwam*
Arabic: *algebra, alcohol, alkali, coffee, giraffe, zero*
Celtic: *bog, clan*
Chinese: *tea*
Dutch: *boss, cookie, snoop, sleigh, stoop* (porch), *yacht*
Finnish: *sauna*
Gaelic: *galore*
German: *dollar, cobalt, kindergarten, quartz, yacht*
Greek: *panorama, paraphernalia, theory, tyrant*
Hebrew: *sapphire, cherub*
Hindi: *bungalow, dungarees, pajama*
Hungarian: *coach, paprika*
Icelandic: *geyser*
Italian: *balcony, mezzanine, opera, umbrella*
Malay: *amok, bamboo*
Maori: *kiwi*
Norwegian: *ski*
Polish: *polka*
Russian: *mammoth*
Swedish: *tungsten*
Tamil: *curry*
Welsh: *coracle, crag*
Yiddish: *bagel, kibitz, lox*

APPENDIX
INTERESTING
ETYMOLOGIES

The most interesting aspect of language to older students is that of word origin, or etymology. There are several ways of approaching this exercise. You can begin by discussing names.

If you have ever visited an English cathedral, you may have noticed a listing of all the deans and bishops since its founding. The early ones are listed simply as John, Peter, Thomas, or Paul with no surnames attached. In the medieval villages the many Johns could be distinguished in four ways:

> by his father: John Peterson. The patronymic is still used routinely in Russia in the male form *Ivanovich* and the female, *Ivanovna* ('son/daughter of Ivan')
> by his occupation: John Miller
> by his dwelling place: John Hill
> by his appearance: John Long (i.e., tall)

In 1399 a poll tax was introduced in England and last names became mandatory; 34 years later, the

Statute of Additions required that last names be stated in all documents. In most instances, people simply used the surname by which they had become known.

These categories of names still exist today. In England and Scandinavia son or sen was added to the father's name, as in Peterson or Petersen. The Scottish used the Celtic Mac as in Macbeth, the Irish Mc as in McIntyre, or o(f) as in O'Donohue, and the French *fils* became *fitz* as in Fitzhugh.

Miller and Smith are the most common English names because they were important medieval occupations—all that wheat needed to be milled into flour for bread, and armor and weapons rusted easily and needed frequent repair and replacement as did farm implements and tools. Incidentally, these trades gave rise to common names in all European languages. And there are other relics of medieval trades— Fletcher ('arrow maker'), Cooper ("barrel maker'), and Forester. Names such as King or Duke originally designated those who served them, e.g., the king's man.

English names derived from distinguishing land-scape features such as Ash (the tree), Brook, Field, Hill, Oak, River, and Stone, abound. North, South, East, and West may have been given to people who moved into a town or village from one of these directions.

Names derived from personal characteristics in-clude Long and Short, Big and Small, Black and White (referring to hair color or complexion). Be-cause many English were of Scandinavian heritage and Scandinavians tended to be blond, White became a common name.

You can categorize the names of some of our presidents. Jackson, Jefferson, Johnson, and Wilson, meant son of; Roosevelt a field of Roses; Ford, just that; -ton as in Clinton, a town; Eisenhower, a hacker of iron (or metal worker); Taylor and Carter are names that reflect the occupations of their forefathers.

A telephone directory is an excellent source for names of all kinds. Because we are a nation of immigrants, discovering the original meaning of names has become complicated and thus all the more challenging to explore.

Of course, first names have meanings too. Phillip means *lover of horses* from the Greek roots *phil* 'love' and *hippos* 'horse.' Thomas means *twin* and Peter *a stone*, both from the Hebrew. Dinah means *vindicated*, Elizabeth, *to whom God is the oath*, and Naomi, *pleasant*—all from the Hebrew.

America is particularly rich in interesting place names. Often the settlers simply named a New World place for a town in their own country. Sometimes they adopted what they thought were the Indian names, and in other cases some incident must have provoked the name. Names of some of our western towns are particularly picturesque in this regard, e.g., Muleshoe, Goodnight, and Truth or Consequences. Many names are simply descriptive, e.g., Sweetwater, Elk Grove, Oak Ridge, or the Tetons (named for their breast-like shape from the French *teton* 'breast').

You can begin a journey of discovery with the days of the week and the months of the year as follows:

Monday—moon day
Tuesday— for Tiew the Norse God
Wednesday—for Wodan or Odin, the chief Norse god
Thursday—for Thor, the Norse god of thunder
Friday— for Frija or Frigga, the wife of Odin
Saturday—for Saturn, a Roman deity, dethroned by his son Jupiter
Sunday—sun day
January— named for Janus, the Roman god of entrances
February—from *februa* 'expiatory offerings' as February 15 marked an important festival of purification, the Lupercalia.
March—for Mars, the Roman god of war
April—the Latin name for the month, related to Latin aprire, 'to open'
May—for the Roman goddess Maia, agricultural deity and mother of Hermes
June—Juno, the wife of Jupiter
July—for Julius Caesar
August —for Augustus Caesar
September, October, November and December were named for the numbers seven to ten as this was the sequence of the Gregorian calendar.

Words from names of people form another interesting group. Some people know about that inveterate gambler, the Earl of Sandwich, who invented the *sandwich* because he did not want to interrupt a winning streak at the gaming table and the nasty English land agent, Captain Boycott, in Ireland who gave rise to the term *boycott*. But there are many others. Colonel Bowie, a defender of the Alamo, gave his name to a knife. *Leotards* are named for a French aerialist, Jules Leotard. The *guillotine* was named for a French physician, Joseph Ignace Guillotin, who, appalled by the suffering caused by inept axemen, invented it, only to become one of its victims. Etienne de Silhouette practiced the then popular art of making cut-out portraits, and the term acquired a wider meaning.

Some words have their origin in superstitions and beliefs. The left side is widely considered unlucky; thus *gauche*, the French word for *left* also means *awkward*, and *sinister* is the Latin word for left. "Left-handed compliment" and "two left feet" are further examples of this very old superstition. By contrast, *right* has long implied correct; *adroit* and *dexterity* are derived from the French and Latin for *right*. The French word for *moon* is *lune*, and a *lunatic* is what you may become if the moon shines on you while you are asleep. *Tadpole* means *toad head* (compare *poll* as in *poll*, or *head*, tax), as it was believed that tadpoles were young toads.

Other words come from images. *Petrified* means turned to stone and *muscle* is a small mouse; have a strong man flex his biceps and you will see why.

Individual words as well as languages have wonderful histories. These little snippets of information can be woven into lessons or introduced when you have a minute left before the bell rings.

APPENDIX
HOW AND WHEN TO
TEACH LATIN
ELEMENTS

Teaching Latin Words

Most Latin-derived words have a particular structure:

PREFIX	+	ROOT	+	CONNECTIVE	+	SUFFIX
in		somn		i		a
ir		reg		ul		ar

In general, the prefix changes meaning and the suffix is a clue to function; e.g., import and export are opposites, but export, exportable, exporter, and exportation represent different grammatical functions. The connective, most often i, occurs only in Latin and Greek words between the root and the suffix. It determines accent; count back one vowel to find the accent, e.g., in som'nia.

We have stopped teaching Latin in most schools, but if SAT scores are ever to stop declining, we have to find a way of teaching the Latin elements that constitute over half the vocabulary of our language.

As soon as students begin to read texts in social studies and science—usually in fourth grade—they encounter many Latin words. We cannot afford to wait until high school to study explanations of Latin elements, and there is every reason to begin earlier. Students benefit greatly from leaving the sixth grade familiar with the more common prefixes and forty or fifty roots, but we can begin even sooner. Young children are at the height of their ability to use language, and we ought to capitalize on that strength before they lose it. Fourth graders are interested in codes, secret and otherwise, and a foreign language is a code.

You can introduce such Latin elements as the prefix *ex-* very early. Even first graders know that the *exit* sign designates the way out of a building, that dinosaurs are *extinct* because they have died out, and that a fire *extinguisher* puts out a fire. By third grade they know that we *export* automobiles, that Jimmy Carter is an *ex-president*, that when you retire you will become an *ex-teacher*, and that you should use *exterior* rather than interior paint on the outside of your house. By fourth grade they should know that "for *external* use only" means you should not eat or drink it, and that crabs have *exoskeletons* and that our bodies *excrete* material.

The same goes for the Latin prefix *pre-*. Elementary students are familiar with the terms *prekindergarten* and *pretests*, and they know what Mom does when she *preheats* the oven, and that if you *predict* rain, you are mentioning it before it happens. But some direct, explicit teaching will lead them to figure out the meaning of more abstract terms, such as *preamble* and *precedent*.

Make cards, and have students make their own sets. The front of the card should contain the Latin element, and the back a really good key word that will evoke the meaning. Just as in beginning reading instruction we use a letter name and give a key word for the sound, e.g., *a apple* /a/, students should read the prefix on the front of the card and then recite the key word, followed by the meaning: *ex - exit - out, con - connect - together*. Some prefixes have two meanings. The prefix *in-* can mean *not* or *into* and the prefix *dis-* can mean *not* or *apart*. Where there are two meanings, two key words will be needed, as *invade - in, insane - not* or *disagree - not, disperse - apart*. Fifth and sixth graders should be familiar with "chameleon" prefixes where the changes, made for reasons of euphony, often affect spelling by giving rise to double letters, e.g., *irregular, illegal, immature*, or *collect, collide*, and *commit*.

As soon as students have mastered a dozen or so prefixes, they can begin to work with roots. Again, begin with the more "transparent" roots whose meanings have not eroded through time: *port* 'to carry,' *ject* 'to throw,' and *rupt* 'to break,' might be a good starting point. Note that Latin roots are verbs.

Roots and prefixes should be added to charts displayed on the wall and to a section in student notebooks. Fourth graders have no difficulty in working with a new root every week. Both direct, explicit teaching and sufficient review to build automaticity are important. Point out to students that Latin usually goes backwards, e.g., *export* is literally "carry out" and *predict* means "say before." Words containing these elements should be read in lists and dictated for reinforcement.

Once students have acquired some familiarity with roots, prefixes, and suffixes, it is time to introduce the concept of the connective, provided that basic decoding skills are in place and students know all their sounds, including consonant and vowel digraphs, and have a good understanding of the six kinds of syllables and of syllabication. There are four so-called Latin connectives (actually an artificial construct, but a useful one). They are *i* (by far the most common), *u*, *ul*, and rarely *ol*. Students should practice circling the connective and marking the accent.

The connectives *u*, *ul*, and *ol* are always pronounced with long vowels: *evaluate, genuine, monument, strenuous, virtuous, muscular, manipulate, opulent, popular, regulate, redolent, somnolent.*

The connective *i* is pronounced /e/ before a vowel (*alleviate, criterion, curious, material, insomnia,*), /i/ before a consonant (*attitude, condiment, substitute*) and /y/ after l or n (*familiar, union*).

Moreover, this same connective *i* combines with a preceding *c*, *t*, *s*, or *x* to create a /sh/ sound, e.g., *artificial, action, expansion,* and *anxious.*

In this situation, it continues to affect accent; the preceding syllable is always accented. Students should practice circling the /sh/ combination and marking the accent.

The rule for the pronunciation of the vowel immediately preceding the /sh/ combination is best taught by having students print the vowels, and then fill them up by doodling. Thus:

$$a \quad e \quad i \quad o \quad u$$

a, *o*, and *u* have the strength to say their names and thus are always long, e.g., *pagination*, *promotion*, and *confusion*.

i is a skinny little thing; it does not have the strength to say its own name, and is always short, e.g., *addition* or *division*.

and *e*, is half full and you have to experiment, e.g., *precious*, but *specious*.

Familiarity with the Latin connective enables students to pronounce correctly words they tend to mispronounce. It is also an aid to spelling; this is particularly true of the connective *i* in its various guises—students who do not know about the connective are prone to such misspellings as *luxureous* or *humileate*.

APPENDIX
HOW TO TEACH
GREEK ELEMENTS

Although Greek roots are best introduced in seventh and eighth grades in preparation for the science vocabulary students will encounter in high school, the Greek code that will enable students to read and spell Greek words can be introduced to fourth graders as follows:

/k/ is usually spelled *ch* as in *school*, *chorus*, *anchor*

/f/ is spelled *ph* as in *phone*, *elephant*, *Philip*

/i/ and /i/ are spelled *y* as in *gym*, *style*, *cyclone*

/z/ is spelled *x* as in *xylophone*, *xylum*

Later you can introduce *p*, silent before *n* and *s*, as in *pneumonia* and *psychology*.

The structure of Greek words in English is a simple one. Two roots, usually nouns (unlike the Latin roots that are verbs) are often combined with an *o* connective in between, e.g., *photograph*, *phono-graph*, or *geography*. In many ways the Greek elements

105

are easier to approach than the Latin ones. You can have fun making posters of Greek roots shaped like a sun with rays. Place the root and its meaning in the center, and write derived words on the rays.

Some of the materials in use for teaching vocabulary combine the Greek and Latin elements of the language in arbitrary listings, but their structure, phonology, and origin are quite different, and they should be taught separately.

Teaching these Latin and Greek elements is crucial for the development of advanced vocabulary now that Latin and Greek studies have declined in our schools and colleges, probably never to be restored to their earlier importance. The world has moved on.

APPENDIX
WORKING WITH
GERMANIC ELEMENTS

What can be done about the Germanic elements of the language which form half of everything in print and, I suspect, are responsible for teachers giving up on phonics and adopting whole language instead? First of all, a few preliminary considerations:

1. Anglo-Saxon words are short; they dropped most of their endings during the Middle English period.

2. Anglo-Saxon tends to have vowel pairs; Latin words do not. Thus, you can be sure that *bread*, *boat* and *sail* are Anglo-Saxon in origin (exceptions are *oi*, *oy*, and *ou* as in *boil*, *loyal*, and *soup*, both sounds adapted from French).

3. Latin seldom has silent letters, but Anglo-Saxon certainly does. In many cases the pronunciation has changed, but the spelling has not. The German word for *knee* is *Knie* and the *k* is pronounced. The *gh* in *light* and *night* was once pronounced like the *ch* in

Scottish *loch*. Exceptions do occur among French- and Latin-derived words, e.g., *autumn*, *debt*, and *doubt*. *Would* and *should* are spelled with an *l* that used to be pronounced (cf. *will* and *shall*); the *l* in *could* was added by analogy.

4. Like German, Anglo-Saxon lends itself to the formation of compound words, e.g., *airport*, *bookcase*, *fireplace*, and *horseback*.

There are reasons for the spelling of all words, even the most non-phonetic. Never tell students, "The English language is just crazy." If you do not know the reason for the spelling of a word, try to find out, and if all else fails, tell your students it probably used to be pronounced that way, and you will often be right.

Germanic words pose problems for reading and even greater ones for spelling. When students read aloud, they often confuse the *th* and *wh* words: *this*, *that*, *these*, *those*, *when*, *where*, *there*, *they*, *them*, *what*, *which*, *how*, *who*, as well as the *ver* words: *over*, *ever*, *even*, *every*. Spelling errors such as *thay* are tough to eradicate. Persistent and systematic efforts are needed.

For reading, teachers should make a pack of cards for daily five-minute drill. Begin with recognition drill. Place no more than four cards on the table and say, "Show me *what*," "Show me *who*," "Show me *where*," "Show me *when*." Then pick up the cards, hold each one up, and test. You can then do a recognition drill with four more, and test with all eight cards. Once students are confident, you can move on to a "quick flash" drill. You can proceed to using cards or strips with the word embodied in a phrase, e.g., "What is that?," "Where are we?," "Who are you?," "When can I go?" Misreading these words creates problems with comprehension, and time invested in drill is not wasted.

Learning to spell these non-phonetic or "red" words correctly takes a lot of practice; they need to be drilled a few at a time over several weeks or even months. They are best taught in groups wherever possible:

to	do does done	carry	any	double
do	go goes gone	marry	many	trouble
		hurry		country
				cousin
other	rough	said	door	push
mother	tough	laid	floor	pull
brother	enough	paid	flood	put

Mnemonic devices can be helpful. Children can learn to spell *eye* by making it into a face. They can distinguish *by* from *buy* by pretending the *u* is a shopping bag. A *friend* is a *friend* to the *end*. *Thorough* is *through* with an *o* stuck in. In *February* you say *brrr* because you are so cold. Encourage students to make up their own mnemonic devices.

Our most powerful memory is the kinesthetic. Words should be written large with markers on old newspapers, on chalkboards, in sand, using simultaneous oral spelling; that is, with students naming the letters as they write. Writing with eyes closed is a good way of sealing the spelling into the memory.

In the case of older students who have fixed spellings such as *thay*, *whith* or *frome* into their motor memories through years of repeated practice, the process of eradicating these apparently "careless" errors is far more difficult. Making a personal spelling pack with words culled from the student's own writing is a good beginning. Cards are better than a list, because they can be sorted and removed as they are mastered. Daily practice over weeks with periodic review may be necessary.

Always we should remember that, while we can teach all students to read up to the level of their intelligence, the same is not true of spelling. There are students who will never learn to spell well enough to profit from a spellcheck that requires at least a fifth-grade spelling level to be useful. Never will I forget a conversation I had with a former student who called to tell me he was enrolled in a graduate program in chemical engineering. In answer to my question about using a computer for his writing, he replied, "Diana, forget it. My spelling never went out of the third grade. A spell check is useless to me!"

APPENDIX
AN APPROACH TO
FRENCH ELEMENTS

As we mentioned earlier, words derived from French are numerous and challenging for both reading and spelling. Consider a couple of phrases: *réspondez s'il vous plait* (generally abbreviated as RSVP) and *parlez vous*. You may correctly conclude that *ez* is pronounced long *a* and the first *e* in *réspondez* also approximates long *a*, but there is no rule to guide you. The *ou* in *vous* is pronounced as in *soup*, and the *s* is silent, as is the *s* in *réspondez*. The *i* in *il* is pronounced as is our long *e*. Not surprisingly, even common French expressions are commonly mispronounced: in *laissez faire* the *ss* should be pronounced like *s*, rather than the *z* commonly heard; *entrepreneur* should rhyme with *her*, not with *your*.

As they entered English, French words often changed their pronunciation without changing the spelling. Often the pronunciation of a French word is determined by the period in which it entered the language. Earlier introductions are more likely to be pronounced as English words; recent introductions retain the French pronunciation. Sometimes you can see a change in process, as in *camouflage* or *nonchalant* where alternate pronunciations are current and accepted.

There are a few principles that can be useful to students.

1. In French-derived words, *ch* is pronounced /sh/: *attaché, brochure, cache, chablis, chaise, chalet, chamois, champagne, chandelier, Chardonnay, chateau, chauffeur, chef, chenille, chic, chiffon, chivalry, chute, douche, machine, nonchalant, parachute, pistachio, sachet.*

However, this does not hold true for words introduced at an earlier stage in the development of the language, such as *attach, avalanche, bachelor, chamber, champion, chance, change, chant, chattel, check,* and *detach.*

2. The digraph *ou* is pronounced /oo/: *accouterment, acoustic, boulevard, caribou, cougar, coupon, detour, limousine, mousse, rouge, roulette, route, routine, sou, soup, souvenir, troupe, trousseau, uncouth, velour, youth.*

3. Final *et, ez,* and accented *e* are usually pronounced approximating our long *a*: *ballet, buffet, chalet, crochet, croquet, filet, sachet, rendezvous, cliché, communiqué, crêpe, crème brulée, entrée, fiancé(e), matinée, melée, passé, risqué.*

4. Final *eau* is pronounced as our long *o*: *beau, bureau, eau de cologne, trousseau.*

5. The French /j/ sound as in *bon jour*, retains its pronunciation in recent introductions such as *beige,*

camouflage, collage, fuselage, garage, genre, lingerie, menage, neglige, protege, prestige, rouge.

In earlier introductions the words became Anglicized and the sound changed to our /j/: *savage, damage, baggage, ravage, marriage, selvage, village.*

6. The digraph *oi/oy* retains its original French pronunciation in some words, e.g., *joie de vivre, reservoir, pâté de fois gras, savoir faire.*

In earlier introductions this is not the case, e.g., *loyal, royal, corduroy, flamboyant, voyage,* (but using the French, we still wish someone a *bon voyage*), *adroit* and *maladroit, gargoyle, clairvoyant.*

7. Both *qu* and *q* are pronounced k: *antique, appliqué, bisque, cheque, clique, communiqué, coq, etiquette, grotesque, mosque, mosquito, oblique, physique, picturesque, pique, technique, unique.*

8. Vowels are pronounced differently in words originating from the French, most notably French *i* is pronounced as long *e*: *chic, cliché, elite, limousine, machine, marine, praline, vis-a-vis.*

The preceding list is by no means complete, but rather serves to illustrate that French words are indeed idiosyncratic for both reading and spelling. They must be taught on a need-to-know basis.

Fortunately, French words are, for the most part, not needed until high school or even college.

APPENDIX
EARTH, FIRE, AND
WATER

Anglo-Saxon	Latin	Greek
earth	*terra*	*gea*
earthworm	*terrain*	*geode*
earthling	*territory*	*geography*
earthenware	*terracotta*	*geometry*
earthworks	*Mediterranean*	*geodesic*
earthly	*terrestrial*	*geophysical*
earthquake	*terrine*	*geopolitical*
earthy	*terrace*	*geocentric*
earthborn	*territorial*	*geology*
earthbound	*terra incognito*	*geomancy*
earthshaking	*terrarium*	*geodetic*
fire	*ignis*	*pyro*
bonfire	*ignite*	*pyre*
firefly	*ignition*	*pyromaniac*
firebomb	*igneous*	*pyrometer*
fireplace	*ignis fatuus*	*pyrotechnics*
fireworks		*pyrite*

fireboat
fireman
firestorm

water	*aqua*	*hydr*
waterfall	*aquatic*	*hydrant*
watery	*aquarium*	*hydraulic*
watercress	*aqualung*	*hydroponic*
watercolor	*aquaculture*	*hydrophone*
watercooler	*aquarelle*	*hydrophobia*
waterfowl	*aquanaut*	*dehydrated*
waterfront	*Aquarius*	*hydrogen*
watermelon	*aqueduct*	*hydra*
watershed	*aquatint*	*hydrocephalus*
watertight	*aquifer*	*hydrofoil*
waterway	*aquavit*	*hydroelectric*
waterlily	*aqueous*	*hydroplane*
watermain	*Aquarian*	*hydrometer*

BIBLIOGRAPHY

Addison, William. 1979. *Understanding English Place-Names*. London: Futura Publications.

Alexander, Michael. 1975. *The Earliest English Poems*. Translated with an introduction by Michael Alexander. Middlesex, England: Penguin Books Ltd.

Bede. 1955. *A History of the English Church and People*. Translated by Sherley-Price. Harmondsworth, Middlesex, England: Penguin classics.

The American Heritage Dictionary of the English Language (3rd ed.). 1992. Boston: Houghton Mifflin Company.

The Anglo-Saxon Chronicle. 1998. Translated and edited by Michael Swanton. New York: Routledge.

Ayers, Donald M. 1986. *English Words from Latin and Greek Elements*. Revised and expanded by Thomas D. Worthen. Tucson: University of Arizona Press.

Ayto, John. 1990. *Dictionary of Word Origins*. New York: Arcade Publishing.

Baker, Timothy. 1966. *The Normans*. New York: Macmillan Co.

Balmuth, Miriam. 1992. *The Roots of Phonics: A Historical Introduction*. Baltimore: York Press.

Barlow, Frank. 1970. *Edward the Confessor*. University of California Press. Berkeley and Los Angeles: University of California Press.

Bryant, Arthur. 1953. *The Story of England: Makers of the Realm*. London: Collins.

Bryson, Bill. 1990. *Mother Tongue: English and How It Got That Way.* New York: Avon Books

Bunyan, John. 1990. *The Pilgrim's Progress.* Hal M. Helms ed. Orleans, MA: Paraclete Press.

Cahill, Thomas. 1995. *How the Irish Saved Civilization: The Untold Story of Ireland's Heroic Role from the Fall of Rome to the Rise of Medieval Europe.* New York: Doubleday.

Chickering, Jr., Howell D. trans. 1977. *Beowulf: A Dual Language Edition.* New York: Bantam Doubleday Dell Publishing Gp.,Inc

The Cambridge Encyclopedia. 1990. Cambridge: Cambridge University Press.

Chambers, W. Walker and John R. Wilkie. 1970. *A Short History of the German Language.* London: Methuen and Co., Ltd.

Chaucer, Geoffrey. 1992. *Canterbury Tales.* New York: Alfred A. Knopf, Inc.

Churchill, Winston S. 1956. *A History of the English Speaking Peoples.* Vol. 1 "The Birth of Britain." New York: Dodd, Mead, & Co.

Claiborne, Robert. 1989. *The Roots of English: A Reader's Handbook of Word Origins.* New York: Times Books.

The Compact Edition of the Oxford English Dictionary. 1971. New York: Oxford University Press.

Crystal, David. 1997. *English as a Global Language.* Cambridge: Cambridge University Press.

Daicher, David. 1960. *A Critical History of English Literature.* Vol. 2. New York: The Ronald Press Co.

Daniell, David. 1994. *Let There Be Light: William Tyndale and the Making of the English Bible.* London: British Library.

Defoe, Daniel. 1930. *Robinson Crusoe.* New York: Heritage Press.

Fromkin, Victoria and Robert Rodman. 1993 (6th ed.) *An Introduction to Language.* New York: Harcourt Brace Jovanovich College Publishers.

Gimbutas, Marija. 1982. *The Goddesses and Gods of Old Europe 6,500-3,500 BC: Myths and Cult Images.* Los Angeles: University of California Press.

Green, Charles. 1988. *Sutton Hoo, The Excavation of a Royal Ship-Burial.* Totowa, NJ: Barnes and Noble Books.

Hartley, Dorothy and Mary Elliot. 1931. *Life and Work of the People of England.* New York: G. P. Putnam's Sons.

Hayakawa, S. I. and Alan R. Hayakawa. 1990. *Language in Thought and Action.* New York: Harcourt Brace Jovanovich College Publishers.

Heaney, Seamus, trans. 2000. *Beowulf: A New Verse Translation.* New York: Farrar, Straus & Girou.

Hibbert, Christopher. 1992. *The Story of England.* London: Phaidon Press Ltd.

The Harvard Classics. 1909. Vol. 15 ed. by Charles W. Eliot. New York: P. F. Collier & Son.

The Holy Bible, King James Version. 1974. New York: Penguin Books USA, Inc.

The Home Book of Modern Verse. Compiled and arranged by Burton Egbert Stevenson. (2nd ed.) 1953. New York: Holt, Rinehart & Winston.

Johnson's Dictionary. A Modern Selection by E. L. McAdam Jr. and George Milne. Toronto: Random House,

Jean, Georges. 1992. *Writing: The Story of Alphabets and Scripts.* New York: Harry N. Abrams, Inc.

Liang, Lloyd and Jennifer. 1990. *Celtic Britain and Ireland AD 200-800: The Myth of the Dark Ages.* New York: St. Martin's Press.

Lyall, Sarah. "Staid Know-It-All Goes Hip and Online." *The New York Times* (Arts Section),10 April, 2000.

Mallory, J. P. 1989. *In Search of the Indo-Europeans: Language, Archeology and Myth.* London: Thames and Hudson, Ltd.

Manguel, Alberto. 1996. *A History of Reading.* New York: Penguin Books USA, Inc.

McCrum, Robert, William Cran, and Robert MacNeil. (eds) 1992. *The Story of English.* New York: Penguin Books USA, Inc.

Mencken, H. L. 1931. *The American Language: An Inquiry into the Development of English in the United States.* New York: Alfred A. Knopf.

The Oxford Book of English Prose. Chosen and edited by Arthur Quiller-Couch. 1925. Oxford: Oxford University Press.

Pei, Mario. 1984. *The Story of Language.* New York: Penguin Books USA, Inc.

Potter, Simeon. 1975. *Language in the Modern World.* London: Andre Deutsch.

_____1957. *Modern Linguistics.* London: Andre Deutsch.

_____1959. *Our Language.* Middlesex: Penguin Books, Ltd.

Pyles, Thomas and John Algeo. 1993. *The Origins and Development of the English Language.* (4th ed.) New York: Harcourt Brace Jovanovich College Publishers.

Spindler, Konrad. 1994. *The Man in the Ice.* Translated from German by Ewald Osers. New York: Harmony Books.

Strunk, William Jr. and White E. B. 1979. *The Elements of Style.* New York: Macmillan.

Swift, Jonathan. 1931. *Gulliver's Travels.* New York: Random House.

Tyndale, William. 1989. *Tyndale's New Testament: A Modern-Spelling Edition of the 1534 Translation* with an introduction by David Daniell. London:Yale University Press.

_____1992. *Tyndale's Old Testament: A Modern-Spelling Edition of the 1534 Translation* with an introduction by David Daniell. London: Yale University Press.

Untermeyer, Louis. A 1942. *Treasury of Great Poems English and American.* New York: Simon & Schuster.

Vallins, G. H. 1954. *Spelling.* With a chapter on American spelling by John W. Clark. London: Andre Deutsch Ltd.

Webster's New Universal Unabridged Dictionary. 1979. (2nd ed.) Cleveland: Simon & Schuster.

Winchester, Simon. 1998. *The Professor and the Madman: A Tale of Murder, Insanity, and the Making of the Oxford English Dictionary.* New York: Harper Collins.

The Anglo-Saxon Heptarchy

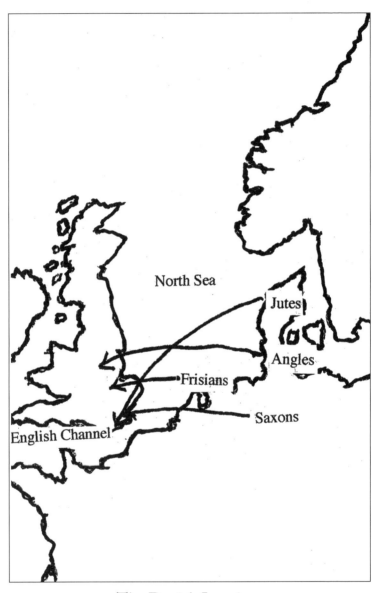

North Sea

Jutes

Angles

Frisians

Saxons

English Channel

The Danish Invasions

England During the Danish Invasions

English Possessions in France Under Henry II